Heart Healthy Cookbook for Beginners 2023

A Collection of 1500+ Delicious, Low-fat and Low-sodium Recipes for Lowering Blood Pressure and Cholesterol Levels. Includes a Flexible 30-Day Meal Plan

Rosalinda Sherman

Table of Contents

Introduction 6

What is a Hearts Disease? 6

Causes and Symptoms of Heart Diseases .. 6

What are the methods for managing heart disease? 7

Who Should Embrace the Heart-Protective Nutrition Pattern 7

Benefits of The Heart Healthy Eating Pattern 8

Heart Healty Diet 9

Strategies for Adhering to the Heart-Healthy Diet 9

Nutrients that Support Cardiovascular Health 10

Foods To Eat for Heart Healthy Eating Pattern 10

Foods To avoid for Heart Healthy Eating Pattern 11

Chapter 1: Breakfast Recipes 12

Delicious Blueberry Smoothie 12

Red Velvet Beet and Cherry Smoothie..... 12

Cheese And Vegetable Frittata 13

Raisin Cashew Oats 13

Muesli with Berries, Seeds, and Nuts 14

Quinoa with Cinnamon and Peaches 15

Strawberry Quinoa Salad 15

Peach-Cranberry Sunrise Muesli 16

Bowl Of Guacamole And Mango With Black Beans 16

Berry Griddle Cakes 17

Broccoli Chicken Rice........................17

Pasta Primavera 18

German Potato Soup 19

Chicken Meatballs 20

Spicy Turkey Wraps 21

Quinoa Vegetable Soup 22

Beet Berry Smoothie 23

Cranberry Hotcakes 23

Chapter 2: Meat Recipes 24

Chicken Shaheata 24

Spiced Beef 25

Slow Roasted Beef 26

Amazing Grilled Chicken and Blueberry Salad 26

Tomato Beef 27

Parmesan Pork Chops 28

Garlic Mushroom Chicken 29

Beef Tenderloin Medallions With Yogurt Sauce..30

Lentil Beef Bolognese.......................30

Chicken with Orzo and Lemon 31

Best Lasagna Soup 32

Sesame Beef Skewers 33

Strip Steak Quinoa 34

Pistachio Flounder Fillets 34

Stewed Cod Filet with Tomatoes.............35

Turkey Keema Curry 36

Basil Pesto Chicken 37

Pineapple Chicken............................37

Chipotle Chicken Lunch Wrap 38

Balsamic Roast Chicken......................39

Tomato Chicken Bake 40

Beef And Vegetable Kebabs 41

Almond Butter Chicken........................41

Chapter 3: Fish and Seafood Recipes 42

Mediterranean Baked Fish......................42

Olive Turkey Patties 43

Orzo, Bean, And Tuna Salad 43

Catfish with Egg Pecans 44

Creamy Tuna Salad 45

Rosemary-Lemon Salmon 45

Roast Salmon with Tarragon 46

Citrus Tilapia 46

Crispy Trout with Herb 46

Pasta with Lemon Spiced Shrimp and Cheese 47

Za'atar Cod Fillets 48

Spicy Shrimp 48

Salmon Patties 49

Chapter 4: Vegetables & Side Dishes 49

Sautéed Spinach with Pumpkin Seeds 49

Zucchini With Cheesy Lasagna 50

Bean Curd Bake 51

Spaghetti Squash with Walnuts and Parmesan 51

Celery With Mushroom Bolognese 52

Spicy Pear Tacos 53

Sesame Spinach 54

Cheese Crepes With Spinach 54

Vegetarian Gyros 55

Umami Mushrooms 56

Creamy Vegetable Quiche 57

Lentils and Rice 58

Cauliflower Mashed "Potatoes" 59

Cannellini Bean Pizza 59

Vegetable Fruit Bowl with Lentil 60

Healthy Banana Cookies With Oatmeal .. 61

Fried Rice Tom Yum 61

Fried Legume 62

Slow Cooker Quinoa Lentil Tacos 63

Butter Bean Penne 64

Chapter 5: Soup Recipes 65

Healthy Bean Soup 65

Veggie Pea Soup 66

Flavors Corn Soup 66

Fruit & Veg Soup 67

Tomato Tofu Soup 68

Potato Squash Soup 69

Silky Zucchini Soup 70

Spicy Bean Soup 70

Flavors Vegetable Stew 71

Butternut Soup 72

Lentil Veggie Stew 73

Homestyle Bean Soup 74

Chapter 6: Snack Recipes 75

Berry Greek Yogurt Parfaits with Granola 75

Hummus 75

Lentil Trail Mix 76

Thyme Mushrooms 76

Honey-Lime Berry Salad 77

Pickled Cucumbers 78

Nutritious Roasted Chickpeas 78

Whipped Ricotta Toast 79

Brussel Sprouts Hummus 80

Curried Cannellini Bean Dip 80

Sikil Peak (Pumpkin Seed Salsa) 81

Cottage Cheese Mousse 81

Oat Nuggets 82

Crispy Carrot Fries 82

Sweet Potato Hummus 83

Lime Wild Rice 83

Cannellini Bean Hummus 84

Spiced Chickpeas With Peppered Parsley 84

Avocado Tomato Salsa 85

Lemon Brussels Sprouts 86

Chapter 7: Desserts Recipes 86

Watermelon Berry Ice Pops 86

Apricot Crisp 87

Baked Apples With Almonds 87

Berries Crumble 88

Honeydew Balsamic Glaze 89

Chocolate Mousse 89

Refreshing Watermelon Ice Pops 90

Berries With Balsamic Vinegar 90

Cookie Cream Shake 91

Strawberry Mint Yogurt 91

Banana Pecan Muffins 92

Baked Apple Slices 92

Creamy Delicious Farro 93

Creamy Fruit Dessert 93

Black Bean Bars 94

Cheddar Cake 95

Brown Rice Pudding................................ 95

Yogurt Cheesecake 96

Banana Cream Nonfat Yogurt 97

Pistachio-Stuffed Dates........................... 97

Meringues With Strawberries, Mint, And Toasted Coconut....................................98

Baked Pear Crisp 98

Strawberry Sorbet 99

Peanut Butter and Chocolate Black Bean Brownie 100

Chocolate "Mousse" With Greek Yogurt And Berries 101

Summer Breezes Smoothie 101

Mascarpone And Honey Figs 102

Hot Cocoa Cup....................................... 102

30-Day Meal Plan....................................... 103

Introduction

What is a Hearts Disease?

Heart disease, also known as cardiovascular disease (CVD), is a health disorder that affects the heart and its functioning. It starts with the accumulation of bad fats, such as cholesterol, in the inner walls of the arteries that supply blood to the heart. This process, called arteriosclerosis, causes the arteries to become thickened and narrowed, which restricts blood flow and increases the risk of heart attack or stroke. Cholesterol is a fatty substance that is found in the body in two forms: HDL and LDL. HDL cholesterol is considered good because it helps to remove cholesterol from the blood and return it to the liver, while LDL cholesterol is considered bad because it sticks to the walls of blood vessels and can block blood flow. CVD is a progressive and chronic condition that requires ongoing management and treatment.

There are many different types of heart disease, including coronary artery disease, heart failure, and arrhythmias. Coronary artery disease is the most common form of CVD and occurs when the arteries that supply blood to the heart become blocked or narrowed due to the buildup of plaque. This can lead to chest pain, also known as angina, or a heart attack. Heart failure is a condition in which the heart is unable to pump enough blood to meet the body's needs. Arrhythmias are abnormal heart rhythms that can cause the heart to beat too fast, too slow, or irregularly.

Risk factors for CVD include high blood pressure, high cholesterol, obesity, smoking, diabetes, and a family history of heart disease. Many of these risk factors can be controlled through lifestyle changes, such as eating a healthy diet, getting regular exercise, and avoiding tobacco products. Medications, such as statins and blood pressure medications, can also be used to lower cholesterol and blood pressure levels. In some cases, surgical procedures may be necessary to treat CVD, such as angioplasty or coronary artery bypass surgery.

It is important to be aware of the signs and symptoms of CVD, which can include chest pain, shortness of breath, palpitations, and fatigue. Seeking medical attention and treatment early on can help to prevent the progression of CVD and reduce the risk of serious complications, such as heart attack or stroke.

Causes and Symptoms of Heart Diseases

Heart disease, also known as cardiovascular disease, is a broad term that refers to a range of conditions that affect the heart and blood vessels. Some of the most common types of heart disease include:

Coronary artery disease: This occurs when the arteries that supply blood to the heart become narrowed or blocked, which can lead to chest pain, heart attack, and other problems.

Heart failure: This occurs when the heart becomes damaged or weak and is unable to pump enough blood to meet the body's needs. Symptoms of heart failure include shortness of breath, fatigue, and swelling in the ankles, feet, and legs.

Heart valve problems: These occur when the valves that regulate the flow of blood through the heart do not function properly. Symptoms may include chest pain, shortness of breath, and a rapid or irregular heartbeat.

Cardiomyopathy: This is a group of conditions that affect the heart muscle, causing it to become thick or enlarged. Symptoms may include shortness of breath, fatigue, and swelling in the ankles, feet, and legs.

Arrhythmias: These are problems with the heart's rhythm that can cause the heart to beat too fast, too slow, or irregularly. Symptoms may include palpitations (a feeling of skipped or extra heartbeats), lightheadedness, and fainting.

There are many potential causes of heart disease, including high blood pressure, high cholesterol, smoking, obesity, diabetes, and a family history of heart disease. It is important to maintain a healthy lifestyle and receive regular check-ups to help prevent the development of heart disease. If you are experiencing symptoms of heart disease, it is important to speak with a healthcare provider for proper diagnosis and treatment.

What are the methods for managing heart disease?

The treatment for heart disease will depend on the specific type and severity of the condition. Some common treatments for heart disease include:

Medications: These may include medications to lower blood pressure, cholesterol, or blood sugar levels, or to thin the blood and prevent clots.

Lifestyle changes: Making healthy lifestyle changes, such as quitting smoking, eating a healthy diet, and getting regular exercise, can help improve heart health and reduce the risk of heart disease.

Surgery: In some cases, surgery may be necessary to treat heart disease. This could include procedures such as angioplasty (to open blocked arteries), bypass surgery (to create a new route for blood flow around a blocked artery), or valve repair or replacement (to fix a malfunctioning heart valve).

Heart procedures: Procedures such as angioplasty, stenting, and coronary artery bypass surgery can help improve blood flow to the heart and reduce the risk of heart attack.

Heart devices: Devices such as pacemakers and implantable cardioverter defibrillators (ICDs) can help regulate the heart's rhythm and prevent arrhythmias.

It is important to work closely with a healthcare provider to determine the best treatment plan for your individual needs. In some cases, a combination of treatments may be necessary to effectively manage heart disease.

Who Should Embrace the Heart-Protective Nutrition Pattern.

The "Heart Healthy Eating Pattern" is a dietary pattern that is recommended by the American Heart Association (AHA) for people who want to improve their cardiovascular health and reduce their risk of heart disease. This pattern emphasizes the consumption of a variety of nutrient-dense foods and limits intake of added sugars, saturated and trans fats, and sodium.

The Heart Healthy Eating Pattern is appropriate for people of all ages who want to improve their heart health, including those who already have heart disease or are at high risk for developing it. This includes individuals who have high blood pressure, high cholesterol, or diabetes, as well as those who are overweight or obese. The Heart Healthy Eating Pattern is also appropriate for people who are generally healthy but want to maintain their good health and reduce their risk of developing heart disease in the future. It is important to note that the Heart Healthy Eating Pattern is not a weight loss diet, but rather a way of eating that is focused on promoting heart health. While following this pattern may help some people lose weight, the primary goal is to improve overall cardiovascular health.

Benefits of The Heart Healthy Eating Pattern

There are several potential benefits of following the Heart Healthy Eating Pattern:

Reducing the risk of heart disease: The Heart Healthy Eating Pattern is designed to reduce the risk of heart disease by promoting the consumption of nutrient-dense foods and limiting intake of unhealthy substances that can contribute to the development of heart disease.

Lowering blood pressure: The Heart Healthy Eating Pattern can help lower blood pressure by limiting intake of sodium and increasing intake of potassium-rich foods, such as fruits and vegetables.

Improving cholesterol levels: The Heart Healthy Eating Pattern can help improve cholesterol levels by limiting intake of saturated and trans fats and increasing intake of monounsaturated and polyunsaturated fats, which are found in foods such as nuts, seeds, and fatty fish.

Promoting weight management: The Heart Healthy Eating Pattern can also help with weight management by encouraging the consumption of nutrient-dense, low-calorie foods and limiting intake of unhealthy, high-calorie foods.

Enhancing overall health: In addition to promoting heart health, the Heart Healthy Eating Pattern can also provide a range of other health benefits, such as improving blood sugar control, reducing the risk of certain types of cancer, and improving digestion and regularity.

Heart Healty Diet

A heart-healthy diet is one that promotes overall health and wellbeing by including a balanced mix of foods from all food groups in the ideal ratios. This includes filling half of your plate with vegetables, a quarter with lean protein, and a quarter with whole grain carbohydrates, as well as incorporating a little healthy fat such as olive oil. This dietary guideline is based on the recommendations of The Mediterranean Diet and The DASH Diet, which focus on low cholesterol and sodium content and an abundance of healthy plant foods like vegetables, fruits, and whole grains.

However, it's important to not only focus on the nutrients that a heart-healthy diet provides, but also to be aware of the potentially harmful ingredients and chemicals that can be found in processed or restaurant foods. To truly nourish your body and eliminate toxic substances, it's often best to cook at home using whole, unprocessed ingredients. While it may be time-consuming, the rewards of home cooking include delicious, flavorful meals that are good for your heart and overall health. Plus, with simple, easy-to-follow recipes, it can be enjoyable and fun to cook at home with the purpose of taking care of your health. Remember, healthy food is good for your heart and beneficial to your body as a whole.

Strategies for Adhering to the Heart-Healthy Diet

Here are some tips and tricks that may help you stick to the Heart Healthy Eating Pattern:

Plan ahead: Planning your meals and snacks in advance can help you make healthier choices and ensure that you have the ingredients on hand to follow the pattern.

Stock up on heart-healthy foods: Keep your pantry and fridge stocked with heart-healthy foods such as fruits, vegetables, whole grains, nuts, seeds, and lean protein sources. This will make it easier for you to follow the pattern when you're busy or in a rush.

Make small, gradual changes: Instead of trying to overhaul your diet all at once, try making small, gradual changes to your eating habits. For example, you could start by swapping out refined grains for whole grains, or adding an extra serving of fruits or vegetables to your meals.

Choose healthier cooking methods: Opt for healthier cooking methods, such as baking, grilling, or sautéing, rather than frying. This will help you reduce your intake of unhealthy fats and calories.

Eat at home more often: Eating at home allows you to have more control over what you're eating and makes it easier to follow the Heart Healthy Eating Pattern. Try to cook at home as often as possible, and bring healthy lunches and snacks to work or school.

Be mindful of portion sizes: Pay attention to portion sizes, as it's easy to overeat even healthy foods if you're not careful. Use measuring cups or a food scale to help you get a better idea of how much you're eating.

Don't be too hard on yourself: It's okay to indulge in your favorite treats every once in a while, as long as you're mostly following the Heart Healthy Eating Pattern. Don't be too hard on yourself if you slip up – just get back on track as soon as you can.

Nutrients that Support Cardiovascular Health

To maintain a healthy heart, it is important to include a variety of nutrients in your diet. These nutrients can help keep your blood cholesterol and blood pressure in check, which can help reduce your risk of heart disease. Some important nutrients to consider incorporating into your diet include soluble fiber, unsaturated fats, potassium, magnesium, and calcium. Each of these nutrients plays a unique role in maintaining healthy cholesterol and blood pressure levels and can be found in a variety of foods such as legumes, oily fish, fruits and vegetables, whole grains, and low fat dairy products.

Soluble fiber is a type of fiber that can help lower cholesterol levels. It is found in legumes, such as beans, lentils, and chickpeas, as well as in fruits, vegetables, and grains like oats. Soluble fiber works by binding to cholesterol in the digestive tract and preventing it from being absorbed into the bloodstream.

Unsaturated fats, especially omega-3 fatty acids, have been shown to be beneficial for cholesterol levels. Good sources of omega-3s include oily fish like salmon, sardines, and mackerel, as well as nuts, seeds, avocado pears, and olive oil. Omega-3s can help lower total cholesterol levels, reduce LDL cholesterol, and increase HDL cholesterol.

Potassium is an essential mineral that helps support healthy blood pressure. It is found in fruits, vegetables, potatoes, whole grain carbohydrates, and avocado pears. Increasing your intake of potassium is one of the benefits of eating more plant-based foods.

Magnesium is a mineral that is involved in many chemical pathways in the body, including the regulation of muscle contraction and relaxation. It helps keep the heartbeat regular and can lower blood pressure. Good sources of magnesium include dark green leafy vegetables, legumes, nuts, and seeds.

Calcium is another mineral that helps regulate muscle contraction and relaxation, as well as maintain the health of arteries. It is important for controlling blood pressure. Food sources of calcium include low fat dairy products, dark green leafy vegetables, almonds, and fish with bones like canned salmon and sardines.

Foods To Eat for Heart Healthy Eating Pattern

The Heart Healthy Eating Pattern emphasizes the consumption of a variety of nutrient-dense foods that are rich in nutrients that support cardiovascular health. These include:

Fruits and vegetables: Aim for at least 4.5 cups of a variety of fruits and vegetables per day. Choose a variety of colors to ensure that you're getting a wide range of nutrients.

Whole grains: Choose whole grain breads, cereals, pasta, and rice instead of their refined counterparts.

Lean protein sources: Choose lean protein sources such as poultry, fish, beans, and tofu. Limit intake of red meat and processed meats.

Nuts and seeds: Nuts and seeds are good sources of heart-healthy fats, fiber, and other nutrients. Try to eat a variety of nuts and seeds, such as almonds, walnuts, flaxseeds, and chia seeds.

Healthy fats: Choose healthy fats such as olive oil, avocado, and nuts instead of unhealthy fats like butter and hydrogenated oils.

Low-fat or fat-free dairy products: Choose low-fat or fat-free milk, cheese, and yogurt to limit your intake of saturated fat.

Plant-based protein sources: Incorporate plant-based protein sources such as beans, lentils, and tofu into your diet.

It's important to also limit your intake of added sugars, saturated and trans fats, and sodium when following the Heart Healthy Eating Pattern.

Foods To avoid for Heart Healthy Eating Pattern

There are certain types of foods that should be limited or avoided when following the Heart Healthy Eating Pattern. These include:

Saturated and trans fats: Foods high in saturated and trans fats should be limited or avoided, as these types of fats can raise cholesterol levels and increase the risk of heart disease. Foods that are high in saturated and trans fats include fried foods, processed meats, and baked goods made with shortening or partially hydrogenated oils.

Sodium: The Heart Healthy Eating Pattern recommends limiting sodium intake to less than 2,300 milligrams (mg) per day. High-sodium foods include processed and packaged foods, such as frozen dinners and snack foods, as well as some types of fast food.

Added sugars: Foods and beverages that are high in added sugars should be limited or avoided, as they can contribute to weight gain and increase the risk of heart disease. Examples of foods high in added sugars include sugary drinks, candy, and sweets.

Refined grains: Choose whole grains over refined grains, as refined grains have been stripped of many of their nutrients and fiber. Examples of refined grains include white bread, pasta, and rice.

It's important to note that it's okay to indulge in your favorite treats every once in a while, as long as you're mostly following the Heart Healthy Eating Pattern. Just be sure to balance these indulgences with plenty of heart-healthy foods.

Chapter 1: Breakfast Recipes

Delicious Blueberry Smoothie

Prep Time: 5 mins, **Servings:** 1, **Cooking Time:** 0 mins

Ingredients

- 1 cup frozen blueberries
- 1 banana, peeled and frozen
- 1/2 cup milk
- 1/2 cup vanilla Greek yogurt
- 1 tsp honey
- 1 tsp vanilla extract

Directions

Combine all ingredients in a blender.

Blend on high until smooth, about 1-2 minutes.

Pour into a glass and enjoy immediately.

Optional additions: a handful of spinach for added nutrients, a scoop of protein powder for added protein, or a splash of orange juice for added flavor.

Nutritional Information: Protein: 8g, Carbohydrate: 27g, Sugar: 21g, Sat Fat: 2g, Fiber: 3g,

Fat: 3g, Calories: 150

Red Velvet Beet and Cherry Smoothie

Prep Time: 5mins, **Servings:** 1, **Cooking Time:** 0mins

Ingredients

- 1 small beet, peeled and chopped
- 1 cup frozen cherries
- 1 scoop vanilla protein powder
- 1 cup unsweetened almond milk
- 1 tsp cocoa powder
- 1 tsp honey (optional)

Directions

Add all ingredients to a blender and blend until smooth. Adjust the sweetness to your preference by adding more honey if desired. Pour into a glass and enjoy immediately.

Nutritional Information: Protein: 18g, Carbohydrate: 37g, Sugar: 25g, Sat Fat: 1g, Fiber: 7g,

Fat: 3g, Calories: 220

Cheese And Vegetable Frittata

Prep Time: 10mins, **Servings:** 4, **Cooking Time:** 20mins

Ingredients

- 8 eggs
- 1/2 cup milk
- 1/2 cup grated cheese (such as cheddar or mozzarella)
- 1 cup diced vegetables (such as bell peppers, onions, and mushrooms)
- 1 tbsp olive oil
- Salt and pepper, to taste

Directions

Preheat the oven to 350°F. In a medium bowl, whisk together the eggs and milk. Stir in the cheese and vegetables.

Heat the olive oil in a large oven-safe skillet over medium heat. Add the egg mixture to the skillet and cook until the edges start to set, about 5 minutes. Transfer the skillet to the oven and bake for 15 minutes, or until the frittata is cooked through and golden brown. Slice and serve.

Nutritional Information: Protein: 20g, Carbohydrate: 5g, Sugar: 3g, Sat Fat: 8g, Fiber: 2g,

Fat: 18g, Calories: 272

Raisin Cashew Oats

Prep Time: 5mins, **Servings:** 1, **Cooking Time:** 5mins

Ingredients

- 1/2 cup old-fashioned oats

- 1 cup water
- 1/4 cup raisins
- 1/4 cup chopped cashews
- 1 tsp honey (optional)

Directions

In a small saucepan, bring the water to a boil. Add the oats and raisins and reduce the heat to low. Cook, stirring occasionally, until the oats are soft and the water is absorbed, about 5 minutes. Stir in the cashews and honey, if using. Serve hot.

Nutritional Information: Protein: 7g, Carbohydrate: 41g, Sugar: 20g, Sat Fat: 3g, Fiber: 5g, Fat: 15g, Calories: 270

Muesli with Berries, Seeds, and Nuts
Prep Time: 10mins, **Servings:** 4, **Cooking Time:** N/A

Ingredients

- 1 cup of rolled oats
- ¼ cup of mixed nuts (almonds, cashews, and peanuts)
- ¼ cup of mixed seeds (sunflower, pumpkin, and sesame)
- 1 cup of mixed berries (strawberries, raspberries, and blueberries)
- ¾ cup of milk or non-dairy milk

Directions

In a large mixing bowl, combine the oats, nuts, seeds, and berries.

Pour in the milk and stir until everything is well combined.

Serve the muesli in bowls and enjoy as is, or top with additional milk or non-dairy milk if desired.

Nutritional Information: Protein: 9g, Carbohydrate: 35g, Sugar: 10g, Sat Fat: 2.5g, Fiber: 6g, Fat: 15g, Calories: 270

Quinoa with Cinnamon and Peaches

Prep Time: 10mins, **Servings:** 4, **Cooking Time:** 20mins

Ingredients

- 1 cup of quinoa
- 2 cups of water
- 1 tsp of cinnamon
- 1 cup of chopped peaches
- 1 tbsp of honey

Directions

Rinse the quinoa in a fine mesh strainer and add it to a pot with the water. Bring the mixture to a boil and then reduce the heat to a simmer. Cover the pot and cook for about 20 minutes or until the quinoa is tender and the water has been absorbed.

Fluff the quinoa with a fork and stir in the cinnamon, peaches, and honey.

Serve the quinoa hot, garnished with additional peaches and a drizzle of honey if desired.

Nutritional Information: Protein: 8g, Carbohydrate: 37g, Sugar: 14g, Sat Fat: 0.5g, Fiber: 4g,

Fat: 2g, Calories: 170

Strawberry Quinoa Salad

Prep Time: 10mins, **Servings:** 4, **Cooking Time:** 20mins

Ingredients

- 1 cup of quinoa
- 2 cups of water
- 1 cup of chopped strawberries
- 1 cup of chopped mixed greens
- 1 tbsp of olive oil
- 1 tbsp of balsamic vinegar

Directions

Rinse the quinoa in a fine mesh strainer and add it to a pot with the water. Bring the mixture to a boil and then reduce the heat to a simmer. Cover the pot and cook for about 20 minutes or until the quinoa is tender and the water has been absorbed.

Fluff the quinoa with a fork and let it cool slightly.

In a large mixing bowl, combine the quinoa, strawberries, mixed greens, olive oil, and balsamic vinegar. Toss until everything is well coated.

Serve the salad chilled or at room temperature.

Nutritional Information: Protein: 6g, Carbohydrate: 22g, Sugar: 4g, Sat Fat: 2g, Fiber: 3g, Fat: 7g, Calories: 150

Peach-Cranberry Sunrise Muesli
Prep Time: 5mins, **Servings:** 1, **Cooking Time:** None

Ingredients

- 1/2 cup rolled oats
- 1/4 cup almond milk
- 1/2 cup diced peaches
- 1/4 cup cranberries
- 1 tbsp honey
- 1 tsp cinnamon
- 1/4 cup chopped almonds

Directions

Combine all ingredients in a bowl and mix well. Serve immediately or cover and refrigerate overnight for a cold breakfast option.

Bowl Of Guacamole And Mango With Black Beans
Prep Time: 10mins, **Servings:** 4, **Cooking Time:** None

Ingredients

- 2 avocados, mashed
- 1 mango, diced
- 1/2 cup black beans, rinsed and drained
- 1/4 cup diced red onion
- 1 tbsp lime juice
- 1 tsp cumin
- 1/4 tsp salt
- 1/4 cup chopped cilantro

Directions

Combine all ingredients in a medium bowl and mix well. Serve immediately with tortilla chips or as a topping for tacos or burritos.

Berry Griddle Cakes

Prep Time: 10mins, **Servings:** 4, **Cooking Time:** 10mins

Ingredients

- 1 cup all-purpose flour
- 1 tsp baking powder
- 1/4 tsp salt
- 1 cup milk
- 1 egg
- 1 tsp vanilla extract
- 1/2 cup mixed berries
- Butter or cooking spray, for griddle
- Maple syrup, for serving (optional)

Directions

In a medium bowl, whisk together flour, baking powder, and salt.

In a separate bowl, whisk together milk, egg, and vanilla extract.

Add wet ingredients to dry ingredients and mix until just combined. Fold in mixed berries.

Heat a griddle or large skillet over medium heat. Coat with butter or cooking spray.

Scoop 1/4 cup of batter onto griddle for each pancake. Cook until bubbles form on the surface, about 2-3 minutes, then flip and cook until the other side is golden brown, about 1-2 more minutes.

Serve hot with maple syrup, if desired.

Broccoli Chicken Rice

Prep Time: 10mins, **Servings:** 4, **Cooking Time:** 30mins

Ingredients:

- 1 cup long grain rice
- 2 cups water

- 1 pound boneless, skinless chicken breasts, cut into bite-size pieces
- 1 tablespoon olive oil
- 1 medium onion, chopped
- 1 red bell pepper, chopped
- 3 cloves garlic, minced
- 1 cup frozen broccoli florets
- 1 teaspoon Italian seasoning
- Salt and black pepper, to taste

Directions:

In a medium saucepan, bring the rice and water to a boil. Reduce the heat to low, cover, and simmer for 20 minutes, or until the rice is tender and the water is absorbed.

In the meantime, heat the oil in a large skillet over medium-high heat. Add the chicken and cook until it is no longer pink, about 5-7 minutes.

Add the onion, bell pepper, and garlic to the skillet and cook for an additional 3-4 minutes, until the vegetables are tender.

Add the broccoli and Italian seasoning to the skillet and cook for an additional 2-3 minutes, until the broccoli is tender.

Season the chicken and vegetable mixture with salt and black pepper, to taste.

Serve the chicken and vegetables over the cooked rice.

Nutritional Information (per serving): Protein: 23g, Carbohydrates: 35g, Sugar: 3g, Sat Fat: 2g, Fiber: 2g, Fat: 6g, Calories: 259

Pasta Primavera

Prep Time: 10mins, **Servings:** 4, **Cooking Time:** 20mins

Ingredients:

- 8 ounces pasta of your choice
- 1 tablespoon olive oil
- 1 medium onion, diced
- 2 cloves garlic, minced
- 1 cup frozen peas
- 1 cup cherry tomatoes, halved
- 1 cup frozen broccoli florets
- 1 cup zucchini, diced
- 1 cup baby spinach
- 1 teaspoon Italian seasoning

- Salt and black pepper, to taste

Directions:

Cook the pasta according to package instructions.

In the meantime, heat the oil in a large skillet over medium-high heat. Add the onion and garlic and cook for 2-3 minutes, until the onion is translucent.

Add the peas, tomatoes, broccoli, zucchini, and spinach to the skillet and cook for an additional 3-4 minutes, until the vegetables are tender.

Add the Italian seasoning, salt, and black pepper to the skillet and stir to combine.

Drain the pasta and add it to the skillet with the vegetables. Toss until the pasta is coated in the vegetable mixture.

Serve the pasta primavera hot.

Nutritional Information (per serving): Protein: 8g, Carbohydrates: 43g, Sugar: 6g, Sat Fat: 2g, Fiber: 4g, Fat: 6g, Calories: 220

German Potato Soup

Prep Time: 15 mins, **Servings:** 6, **Cooking Time:** 1 hour

Ingredients

- 2 lbs potatoes, peeled and diced
- 1 large onion, diced
- 1 carrot, diced
- 1 celery stalk, diced
- 4 cups chicken broth
- 1 cup water
- 1 tsp salt
- 1 tsp pepper
- 1 tsp paprika
- 1 bay leaf
- 1 cup milk or heavy cream
- 2 tbsp butter

Directions

In a large pot, heat the butter over medium heat. Add the onion, carrot, and celery and cook for 5 minutes until the vegetables are softened.

Add the potatoes, chicken broth, water, salt, pepper, paprika, and bay leaf to the pot. Bring to a boil, then reduce the heat to low and simmer for 45 minutes or until the potatoes are tender.

Remove the bay leaf and blend the soup using an immersion blender until it is smooth.

Stir in the milk or cream and heat until the soup is hot.

Serve the soup hot with a sprinkle of paprika on top, if desired.

Nutritional Information: Protein: 6g, Carbohydrate: 24g, Sugar: 5g, Sat Fat: 6g, Fiber: 3g, Fat: 8g, Calories: 214

Chicken Meatballs

Prep Time: 15 mins, **Servings:** 6, **Cooking Time:** 20 mins

Ingredients

- 1 lb ground chicken
- 1 egg, beaten
- ¼ cup breadcrumbs
- 1 tbsp chopped parsley
- 1 tsp garlic powder
- 1 tsp onion powder
- 1 tsp salt
- 1 tsp pepper
- 1 tbsp olive oil

Directions

In a large bowl, mix together the ground chicken, egg, breadcrumbs, parsley, garlic powder, onion powder, salt, and pepper until well combined.

Shape the mixture into small meatballs, about the size of a golf ball.

Heat the olive oil in a large skillet over medium heat. Add the meatballs and cook for about 10 minutes, turning occasionally, until they are cooked through and browned on all sides.

Serve the meatballs hot, with your choice of sauce or dipping sauce.

Nutritional Information: Protein: 21g, Carbohydrate: 6g, Sugar: 0g, Sat Fat: 3g, Fiber: 0g, Fat: 11g, Calories: 214

Spicy Turkey Wraps

Prep Time: 10mins, **Servings:** 4, **Cooking Time:** 10mins

Ingredients

- 1 pound ground turkey
- 1 tablespoon olive oil
- 1 teaspoon chili powder
- 1 teaspoon cumin
- 1/2 teaspoon paprika
- 1/4 teaspoon garlic powder
- 1/4 teaspoon onion powder
- 1/4 teaspoon salt
- 1/4 teaspoon black pepper
- 4 wraps or tortillas
- 1 cup shredded lettuce
- 1 cup diced tomato
- 1 cup shredded cheese
- 1/2 cup diced onion
- 1/2 cup diced bell pepper
- 1/2 cup diced avocado
- 1/2 cup diced jalapeno
- 1/4 cup diced cilantro

Directions

Heat a large skillet over medium-high heat. Add the ground turkey and cook until browned, breaking it up into small pieces as it cooks.

In a small bowl, mix together the olive oil, chili powder, cumin, paprika, garlic powder, onion powder, salt, and black pepper. Pour the spice mix over the ground turkey and stir to coat.

Place a wrap on a flat surface and top with lettuce, tomato, cheese, onion, bell pepper, avocado, jalapeno, and cilantro.

Add a spoonful of the spicy ground turkey onto the wrap and roll it up tightly. Repeat with the remaining wraps.

Heat a large skillet over medium heat. Place the wraps seam-side down in the skillet and cook for 2-3 minutes on each side, or until crispy and golden brown.

Serve immediately.

Nutritional Information (per serving): Protein: 24g, Carbohydrate: 24g, Sugar: 6g, Sat Fat: 6g, Fiber: 6g, Fat: 24g, Calories: 324

Quinoa Vegetable Soup

Prep Time: 10mins, **Servings:** 4, **Cooking Time:** 30mins

Ingredients

- 1 tablespoon olive oil
- 1 medium onion, diced
- 2 cloves garlic, minced
- 1 cup quinoa, rinsed
- 1 quart vegetable broth
- 1 cup water
- 1 cup diced carrots
- 1 cup diced bell peppers
- 1 cup frozen peas
- 1 cup diced tomatoes
- 1 teaspoon dried basil
- 1 teaspoon dried oregano
- 1/2 teaspoon salt
- 1/4 teaspoon black pepper

Directions

Heat the olive oil in a large pot over medium heat. Add the onion and garlic and cook until the onion is translucent, about 5 minutes.

Add the quinoa, vegetable broth, water, carrots, bell peppers, peas, tomatoes, basil, oregano, salt, and black pepper to the pot. Bring the mixture to a boil.

Reduce the heat to low and simmer for 20 minutes, or until the quinoa is cooked and the vegetables are tender.

Serve the soup hot.

Nutritional Information (per serving): Protein: 8g, Carbohydrate: 22g, Sugar: 6g, Sat Fat: 1g, Fiber: 4g, Fat: 3g, Calories: 148

Beet Berry Smoothie

Prep Time: 5 mins, **Servings:** 1, **Cooking Time:** 0 mins

Ingredients:

- 1 small cooked beet, chopped
- 1 cup frozen mixed berries
- 1 banana
- 1 cup almond milk
- 1 tbsp honey

Directions:

In a blender, combine the cooked beet, frozen berries, banana, almond milk, and honey.

Blend until smooth and creamy.

Pour into a glass and serve immediately.

Nutritional Information: Protein: 3g, Carbohydrate: 37g, Sugar: 25g, Sat Fat: 0g, Fiber: 6g, Fat: 2g, Calories: 162

Cranberry Hotcakes

Prep Time: 10 mins, **Servings:** 4, **Cooking Time:** 15 mins

Ingredients:

- 1 cup all-purpose flour
- 2 tsp baking powder
- 1 tsp sugar
- ¼ tsp salt
- 1 cup milk
- 1 egg
- 1 tbsp unsalted butter, melted
- 1 cup fresh cranberries

Directions:

In a bowl, whisk together the flour, baking powder, sugar, and salt.

In a separate bowl, whisk together the milk and egg.

Add the wet ingredients to the dry ingredients and stir until just combined.

Gently fold in the cranberries.

Heat a griddle or large pan over medium heat.

Scoop ¼ cup of the pancake batter onto the griddle for each pancake.

Cook for 2-3 minutes on each side, or until the edges start to look dry and the surface of the pancake has some bubbles.

Repeat with the remaining batter and serve immediately.

Nutritional Information: Protein: 7g, Carbohydrate: 47g, Sugar: 12g, Sat Fat: 7g, Fiber: 2g, Fat: 8g, Calories: 259

Chapter 2: Meat Recipes

Chicken Shaheata

Prep Time: 20mins, **Servings:** 4, **Cooking Time:** 45mins

Ingredients

- 4 chicken breasts, cut into bite-sized pieces
- 1 cup Greek yogurt
- 1 lemon, juiced
- 2 cloves garlic, minced
- 1 teaspoon ground cumin
- 1 teaspoon ground coriander
- 1 teaspoon paprika
- 1 teaspoon turmeric
- 1 teaspoon salt
- 1 tablespoon olive oil

Directions

In a small bowl, mix together the yogurt, lemon juice, garlic, cumin, coriander, paprika, turmeric, and salt. Place the chicken in a large bowl and pour the yogurt mixture over the top. Toss to coat the chicken evenly.

Heat the olive oil in a large skillet over medium-high heat. Add the chicken and cook for 8-10 minutes, or until cooked through.

Serve the chicken with rice or couscous and your choice of vegetables.

Nutritional Information: Protein: 31g, Carbohydrate: 7g, Sugar: 3g, Sat Fat: 2g, Fiber: 1g, Fat: 7g, Calories: 251

Spiced Beef

Prep Time: 10mins, **Servings:** 4, **Cooking Time:** 1 hour

Ingredients

- 2 lbs beef chuck roast
- 1 tablespoon olive oil
- 1 onion, diced
- 2 cloves garlic, minced
- 1 teaspoon ground cumin
- 1 teaspoon ground coriander
- 1 teaspoon paprika
- 1 teaspoon chili powder
- 1 teaspoon salt
- 1 cup beef broth
- 1 can (14.5 ounces) diced tomatoes

Directions

Preheat your oven to 3750F. Heat the olive oil in a large skillet over medium-high heat. Add the beef and cook for 3-4 minutes on each side, or until browned.

Remove the beef from the skillet and place it in a large baking dish. In the same skillet, add the onion and cook for 2-3 minutes, or until translucent. Add the garlic and cook for an additional minute.

Add the cumin, coriander, paprika, chili powder, and salt to the skillet and stir to combine. Pour in the beef broth and diced tomatoes and bring the mixture to a simmer.

Pour the tomato mixture over the beef in the baking dish. Cover the dish with foil and roast for 1 hour, or until the beef is tender.

Serve the beef with rice or potatoes and your choice of vegetables.

Nutritional Information: Protein: 37g, Carbohydrate: 10g, Sugar: 5g, Sat Fat: 9g, Fiber: 2g, Fat: 14g, Calories: 358

Slow Roasted Beef

Prep Time: 10mins, **Servings:** 8, **Cooking Time:** 4 hours

Ingredients

- 3 lbs beef chuck roast
- 1 tablespoon olive oil
- 1 onion, diced
- 2 cloves garlic, minced
- 1 teaspoon salt
- 1 teaspoon black pepper
- 1 cup beef broth
- 1 cup red wine

Directions

Preheat your oven to 2750F. Heat the olive oil in a large skillet over medium-high heat. Add the beef and cook for 3-4 minutes on each side, or until browned.

Remove the beef from the skillet and place it in a large baking dish. In the same skillet, add the onion and cook for 2-3 minutes, or until translucent. Add the garlic and cook for an additional minute.

Pour the beef broth and red wine over the beef in the baking dish. Season the beef with salt and pepper.

Cover the dish with foil and roast

Amazing Grilled Chicken and Blueberry Salad

Prep Time: 20mins, **Servings:** 4, **Cooking Time:** 10mins

Ingredients

- 1 lb of boneless, skinless chicken breasts
- 1 pint of fresh blueberries
- 1/2 cup of crumbled feta cheese
- 1/4 cup of chopped walnuts
- 1/4 cup of sliced red onions
- 1/4 cup of balsamic vinegar
- 1/4 cup of olive oil
- 1 tbsp of honey
- 1 tsp of Dijon mustard
- Salt and pepper, to taste

Directions

Preheat grill to medium-high heat. Season chicken with salt and pepper. Grill chicken for 6-8 minutes on each side, or until cooked through. Let the chicken rest for 5 minutes before slicing.

In a small bowl, whisk together balsamic vinegar, olive oil, honey, and Dijon mustard. Season with salt and pepper.

In a large bowl, combine sliced chicken, blueberries, feta cheese, walnuts, and red onions. Drizzle with dressing and toss to coat.

Serve immediately.

Nutritional Information: Protein: 31g, Carbohydrate: 16g, Sugar: 12g, Sat Fat: 7g, Fiber: 2g,

Fat: 23g, Calories: 375

Tomato Beef

Prep Time: 15mins, **Servings:** 4, **Cooking Time:** 30mins

Ingredients

- 1 lb of ground beef
- 1 can of diced tomatoes
- 1 medium onion, diced
- 1 cup of beef broth
- 1 tsp of garlic powder
- 1 tsp of dried oregano
- 1 tsp of dried basil
- 1 tsp of paprika
- 1 tsp of salt
- 1/2 tsp of black pepper
- 1/2 cup of uncooked quinoa
- 1/2 cup of uncooked brown rice
- 1/4 cup of tomato sauce

Directions

In a large skillet, cook ground beef over medium heat until browned. Drain excess fat.

Add diced tomatoes, onion, beef broth, garlic powder, oregano, basil, paprika, salt, and pepper to the skillet. Stir to combine.

Add quinoa, brown rice, and tomato sauce to the skillet. Stir to combine.

Bring the mixture to a boil, then reduce heat to low and simmer for 20-25 minutes, or until the quinoa and rice are cooked.

Serve immediately.

Nutritional Information: Protein: 25g, Carbohydrate: 35g, Sugar: 6g, Sat Fat: 5g, Fiber: 4g, Fat: 8g, Calories: 309

Parmesan Pork Chops

Prep Time: 15mins, **Servings:** 4, **Cooking Time:** 20mins

Ingredients

- 4 boneless pork chops
- 1/2 cup of grated Parmesan cheese
- 1/2 cup of breadcrumbs
- 1 tsp of garlic powder
- 1 tsp of dried oregano
- 1 tsp of dried basil
- 1 tsp of paprika
- 1/2 tsp of salt
- 1/2 tsp of black pepper
- 2 tbsp of olive oil

Directions

Preheat oven to 400°F.

In a small bowl, mix together Parmesan cheese, breadcrumbs, garlic powder, oregano, basil, paprika, salt, and pepper.

Brush both sides of the pork chops with olive oil. Press the breadcrumb mixture onto both sides of the pork chops, pressing gently to help it stick.

Place the pork chops on a baking sheet and bake for 20 minutes, or until the internal temperature reaches 145°F.

Serve immediately.

Nutritional Information (per serving): Calories: 335, Fat: 20g, Saturated Fat: 6g, Cholesterol: 94mg, Sodium: 679mg, Carbohydrates: 13g, Fiber: 1g, Sugar: 1g, Protein: 30g

Garlic Mushroom Chicken

Prep Time: 10mins, **Servings:** 4, **Cooking Time:** 20mins

Ingredients

- 1 pound boneless, skinless chicken breasts
- 1 tablespoon olive oil
- 8 ounces sliced mushrooms
- 3 cloves garlic, minced
- 1 teaspoon Italian seasoning
- Salt and pepper, to taste
- 1/2 cup chicken broth
- 2 tablespoons butter
- 2 tablespoons chopped fresh parsley

Directions

In a large skillet over medium-high heat, heat oil. Add chicken and cook until browned, about 3-4 minutes per side.

Remove chicken from skillet and set aside.

In the same skillet, add mushrooms and garlic and cook until mushrooms are tender, about 5 minutes.

Stir in Italian seasoning, salt, and pepper.

Add chicken broth and bring to a simmer.

Add the chicken back to the skillet and cover. Reduce heat to low and simmer for about 10 minutes or until the chicken is cooked through.

Remove the chicken from the skillet and set aside.

Add butter to the skillet and let it melt. Stir in parsley and cook for an additional minute.

Slice the chicken and serve with the garlic mushroom sauce.

Nutritional Information: Protein: 30g, Carbohydrate: 5g, Sugar: 1g, Sat Fat: 7g, Fiber: 1g, Fat: 13g, Calories: 270

Beef Tenderloin Medallions With Yogurt Sauce

Prep Time: 10mins, **Servings:** 4, **Cooking Time:** 20mins

Ingredients

- 1 pound beef tenderloin medallions
- 1 tablespoon olive oil
- Salt and pepper, to taste
- 1/2 cup plain Greek yogurt
- 1 tablespoon Dijon mustard
- 1 clove garlic, minced
- 1 teaspoon chopped fresh dill

Directions

In a large skillet over medium-high heat, heat oil.

Season the beef medallions with salt and pepper.

Add the beef to the skillet and cook for 2-3 minutes per side or until desired doneness is reached.

Remove the beef from the skillet and set aside.

In a small bowl, mix together the yogurt, mustard, garlic, and dill.

Slice the beef and serve with the yogurt sauce on top.

Nutritional Information: Protein: 31g, Carbohydrate: 2g, Sugar: 2g, Sat Fat: 6g, Fiber: 0g, Fat: 13g, Calories: 250

Lentil Beef Bolognese

Prep Time: 10mins, **Servings:** 4, **Cooking Time:** 30mins

Ingredients

- 1 tablespoon olive oil
- 1 pound ground beef
- 1 onion, diced
- 2 cloves garlic, minced
- 1 cup lentils, cooked
- 1 (14.5 ounce) can diced tomatoes
- 1 tablespoon tomato paste
- 1 teaspoon Italian seasoning

- Salt and pepper, to taste
- 1/2 cup beef broth
- 1/4 cup grated Parmesan cheese

Directions

In a large saucepan over medium heat, heat oil.

Add the ground beef and cook until browned, about 5 minutes.

Add the onion and garlic and cook until the onion is translucent, about 3 minutes.

Stir in the cooked lentils, diced tomatoes, tomato paste, Italian seasoning, salt, and pepper.

Add the beef broth and bring to a simmer.

Simmer for 20 minutes or until the sauce has thickened.

Stir in the Parmesan cheese.

Serve over pasta or with a side of your choice.

Nutritional Information: Protein: 28g, Carbohydrate: 26g, Sugar: 7g, Sat Fat: 6g

Chicken with Orzo and Lemon

Prep Time: 15 mins, **Servings:** 4, **Cooking Time:** 30 mins

Ingredients:

- 1 pound orzo
- 1 pound boneless, skinless chicken breasts, cut into 1-inch pieces
- 1 teaspoon olive oil
- 2 cloves garlic, minced
- 1 lemon, zested and juiced
- 1/2 cup chicken broth
- 1/4 cup heavy cream
- 1/4 cup chopped fresh parsley
- Salt and pepper, to taste

Directions:

Cook orzo according to package instructions.

In a separate pan, heat the olive oil over medium-high heat. Add the chicken and cook until it is browned on all sides and cooked through, about 5-7 minutes.

Add the garlic to the pan with the chicken and cook for an additional minute.

Add the lemon zest, lemon juice, chicken broth, and heavy cream to the pan. Bring the mixture to a boil, then reduce the heat to a simmer.

Add the cooked orzo to the pan with the chicken and stir to combine.

Add the chopped parsley and season with salt and pepper, to taste.

Serve hot and enjoy!

Nutritional Information: Protein: 26g, Carbohydrate: 47g, Sugar: 2g, Sat Fat: 5g, Fiber: 3g, Fat: 8g, Calories: 366

Best Lasagna Soup

Prep Time: 10 mins, **Servings:** 6, **Cooking Time:** 30 mins

Ingredients:

- 1 pound ground beef
- 1 onion, diced
- 2 cloves garlic, minced
- 2 tablespoons tomato paste
- 1 (28-ounce) can crushed tomatoes
- 4 cups beef broth
- 1 teaspoon Italian seasoning
- 1/2 teaspoon salt
- 1/4 teaspoon black pepper
- 8 uncooked lasagna noodles, broken into small pieces
- 1 cup ricotta cheese
- 1 cup shredded mozzarella cheese
- 1/4 cup grated parmesan cheese
- 1/4 cup chopped fresh basil

Directions:

In a large pot, cook the ground beef over medium heat until it is browned and no longer pink. Add the onion and garlic and cook for an additional 5 minutes.

Add the tomato paste, crushed tomatoes, beef broth, Italian seasoning, salt, and pepper to the pot. Bring the mixture to a boil, then reduce the heat to a simmer.

Add the broken lasagna noodles to the pot and simmer until the noodles are cooked, about 10-15 minutes.

Stir in the ricotta cheese, mozzarella cheese, and parmesan cheese.

Garnish with chopped basil and serve hot.

Nutritional Information: Protein: 28g, Carbohydrate: 32g, Sugar: 6g, Sat Fat: 14g, Fiber: 3g, Fat: 25g, Calories: 438

Sesame Beef Skewers

Prep Time: 20 mins, **Servings:** 4, **Cooking Time:** 15 mins

Ingredients:

- 1 pound beef sirloin, cut into 1-inch cubes
- 1/4 cup low-sodium soy sauce
- 2 tablespoons honey
- 2 cloves garlic, minced
- 1 tablespoon sesame oil
- 1 teaspoon grated ginger
- 1/2 teaspoon red pepper flakes
- 1/4 cup sesame seeds
- 1 green bell pepper, cut into 1-inch pieces
- 1 red bell pepper, cut into 1-inch pieces
- 1 small red onion, cut into 1-inch pieces
- Salt and pepper, to taste

Directions:

In a small bowl, whisk together the soy sauce, honey, garlic, sesame oil, ginger, and red pepper flakes.

Thread the beef cubes onto skewers, along with the bell peppers and onion. Season with salt and pepper.

Heat a grill or grill pan over medium-high heat. Grill the skewers for about 5-7 minutes per side, or until the beef is cooked to your desired level of doneness.

Brush the skewers with the soy sauce mixture and sprinkle with sesame seeds. Grill for an additional 2 minutes, or until the sesame seeds are toasted.

Serve hot and enjoy!

Nutritional Information: Protein: 26g, Carbohydrate: 15g, Sugar: 10g, Sat Fat: 3g, Fiber: 2g, Fat: 12g, Calories: 259

Strip Steak Quinoa

Prep Time: 10 mins, **Servings:** 4, **Cooking Time:** 20 mins

Ingredients:

- 1 pound strip steak
- 1 cup quinoa, rinsed and drained
- 2 cups water
- 1/2 teaspoon salt
- 1/4 cup olive oil
- 1 lemon, juiced
- 2 cloves garlic, minced
- 1/4 cup chopped fresh parsley
- Salt and pepper, to taste

Directions:

Heat a grill or grill pan over high heat. Season the strip steak with salt and pepper and grill for about 4-5 minutes per side, or until it is cooked to your desired level of doneness.

In a small saucepan, bring the quinoa, water, and salt to a boil. Reduce the heat to a simmer and cook until the quinoa is tender, about 15-20 minutes.

In a small bowl, whisk together the olive oil, lemon juice, garlic, and parsley. Season with salt and pepper.

Slice the steak into thin strips and serve over the cooked quinoa. Drizzle with the lemon-parsley dressing and enjoy!

Nutritional Information: Protein: 30g, Carbohydrate: 34g, Sugar: 1g, Sat Fat: 6g, Fiber: 3g, Fat: 16g, Calories: 411

Pistachio Flounder Fillets

Prep Time: 15mins, **Servings:** 4, **Cooking Time:** 15mins

Ingredients

- 4 flounder fillets
- 1/2 cup shelled pistachios, finely chopped
- 1/4 cup bread crumbs
- 1/4 cup grated Parmesan cheese
- 1 tablespoon lemon zest
- 1 teaspoon dried basil

- 1/2 teaspoon garlic powder
- 1/4 teaspoon salt
- 1/4 teaspoon black pepper
- 1 egg, beaten
- 1 tablespoon olive oil

Directions

In a shallow dish, mix together the pistachios, bread crumbs, Parmesan cheese, lemon zest, basil, garlic powder, salt, and pepper.

Brush the fillets with the beaten egg.

Press the fillets into the pistachio mixture to coat both sides.

Heat a large skillet over medium heat and add the olive oil.

Once the oil is hot, add the fillets and cook for 4-5 minutes on each side, or until they are golden brown and cooked through.

Serve immediately.

Nutritional Information: Protein: 26g, Carbohydrate: 10g, Sugar: 2g, Sat Fat: 4g, Fiber: 2g,

Fat: 18g, Calories: 298

Stewed Cod Filet with Tomatoes

Prep Time: 10mins, **Servings:** 4, **Cooking Time:** 20mins

Ingredients

- 1 pound cod filet, cut into large chunks
- 1 tablespoon olive oil
- 1 onion, chopped
- 2 cloves garlic, minced
- 1 (14.5 ounce) can diced tomatoes
- 1/4 cup white wine
- 1/4 teaspoon salt
- 1/4 teaspoon black pepper
- 1/4 teaspoon dried oregano
- 1/4 teaspoon dried basil
- 1/4 cup chopped fresh parsley

Directions

Heat a large skillet over medium heat and add the olive oil.

Once the oil is hot, add the onion and garlic and cook until the onion is translucent.

Add the cod chunks and cook for 2-3 minutes on each side, or until they are lightly browned.

Add the tomatoes, white wine, salt, pepper, oregano, and basil.

Bring the mixture to a simmer and cook for an additional 5-10 minutes, or until the cod is cooked through.

Stir in the parsley and serve immediately.

Nutritional Information: Protein: 25g, Carbohydrate: 10g, Sugar: 4g, Sat Fat: 2g, Fiber: 2g, Fat: 7g, Calories: 170

Turkey Keema Curry

Prep Time: 15 mins, **Servings:** 4, **Cooking Time:** 20 mins

Ingredients:

- 1 tbsp vegetable oil
- 1 onion, finely chopped
- 2 cloves garlic, minced
- 1 tsp grated ginger
- 1 lb ground turkey
- 1 tsp garam masala
- 1 tsp cumin
- 1 tsp coriander
- 1 tsp paprika
- 1 cup tomato sauce
- 1 cup water
- 1 cup frozen peas
- Salt, to taste

Directions:

In a large saucepan, heat the oil over medium heat.

Add the onion, garlic, and ginger and cook until the onion is soft and translucent, about 5 minutes.

Add the ground turkey and cook until it is no longer pink, breaking it up with a wooden spoon as it cooks.

Stir in the garam masala, cumin, coriander, and paprika and cook for 1 minute.

Add the tomato sauce and water and bring to a boil.

Reduce the heat to low and simmer for 10 minutes.

Stir in the frozen peas and simmer for an additional 5 minutes.

Season with salt to taste and serve hot.

Nutritional Information: Protein: 25g, Carbohydrate: 12g, Sugar: 6g, Sat Fat: 7g, Fiber: 3g, Fat: 14g, Calories: 249

Basil Pesto Chicken

Prep Time: 10 mins, **Servings:** 4, **Cooking Time:** 20 mins

Ingredients:

- 4 boneless, skinless chicken breasts
- Salt, to taste
- Pepper, to taste
- 1 cup basil pesto
- 1 cup cherry tomatoes, halved
- 4 tbsp grated Parmesan cheese

Directions:

Preheat the oven to 400°F and line a baking sheet with parchment paper.

Season the chicken breasts with salt and pepper on both sides.

Spread 2 tbsp of basil pesto over each chicken breast.

Top with cherry tomato halves and sprinkle with Parmesan cheese.

Bake for 20 minutes, or until the chicken is cooked through and the cheese is melted and golden brown.

Serve hot with additional pesto on the side, if desired.

Pineapple Chicken

Prep Time: 10 mins, **Servings:** 4, **Cooking Time:** 20 mins

Ingredients:

- 4 boneless, skinless chicken breasts

- Salt, to taste
- Pepper, to taste
- 1 cup pineapple chunks
- 1 cup cherry tomatoes, halved
- 2 tbsp olive oil
- 2 tbsp honey
- 1 tbsp soy sauce
- 1 tsp grated ginger
- 1 clove garlic, minced
- 2 green onions, thinly sliced

Directions:

Preheat the oven to 400°F and line a baking sheet with parchment paper.

Season the chicken breasts with salt and pepper on both sides.

In a small bowl, whisk together the olive oil, honey, soy sauce, ginger, and garlic.

Place the chicken breasts on the prepared baking sheet and brush with the honey mixture.

Top the chicken with pineapple chunks and cherry tomatoes.

Bake for 20 minutes, or until the chicken is cooked through and the pineapple is caramelized.

Sprinkle with green onions and serve hot.

Nutritional Information: Protein: 31g, Carbohydrate: 23g, Sugar: 21g, Sat Fat: 3g, Fiber: 2g, Fat: 9g, Calories: 259

Chipotle Chicken Lunch Wrap

Prep Time: 10 mins, **Servings:** 4, **Cooking Time:** 0 mins

Ingredients:

- 4 whole wheat tortillas
- 1 cup cooked and shredded chicken
- ¼ cup mayonnaise
- 2 tbsp chipotle peppers in adobo sauce
- 1 cup shredded lettuce
- 1 cup diced tomato
- 1 avocado, sliced

Directions:

In a small bowl, mix together the chicken, mayonnaise, and chipotle peppers in adobo sauce.

Lay the tortillas on a flat surface and divide the chicken mixture among them, spreading it evenly over the center of each tortilla.

Top the chicken with lettuce, tomato, and avocado slices.

Roll the tortillas tightly around the filling and cut them in half.

Serve the wraps immediately, or wrap them in plastic wrap and refrigerate until ready to eat

Balsamic Roast Chicken

Prep Time: 10 mins, **Servings:** 4, **Cooking Time:** 1 hr

Ingredients:

- 1 whole chicken (3-4 lbs)
- 1 cup balsamic vinegar
- 1 cup chicken broth
- 1 tbsp honey
- 2 cloves garlic, minced
- 1 tsp dried oregano
- 1 tsp dried basil
- Salt, to taste
- Pepper, to taste

Directions:

Preheat the oven to 350°F.

In a small saucepan, combine the balsamic vinegar, chicken broth, honey, garlic, oregano, and basil.

Bring the mixture to a boil, then reduce the heat and simmer for 10 minutes, or until it has reduced and thickened slightly.

Season the chicken with salt and pepper on both sides.

Place the chicken in a roasting pan and pour the balsamic mixture over the top.

Roast the chicken for 1 hour, or until it is cooked through and the internal temperature reaches 165°F.

Baste the chicken with the pan juices every 20 minutes while it is cooking.

Serve the chicken hot, with the pan juices spooned over the top.

Nutritional Information: Protein: 37g, Carbohydrate: 12g, Sugar: 10g, Sat Fat: 3g, Fiber: 0g, Fat: 9g, Calories: 256

Tomato Chicken Bake

Prep Time: 10 mins, **Servings:** 4, **Cooking Time:** 30 mins

Ingredients:

- 4 chicken breasts
- 1 cup diced tomatoes
- 1 cup mozzarella cheese, shredded
- 1 cup breadcrumbs
- 1 tsp dried oregano
- 1 tsp dried basil
- Salt, to taste
- Pepper, to taste
- 1 tbsp olive oil

Directions:

Preheat the oven to 400°F.

Place the chicken breasts in a baking dish.

Top the chicken with diced tomatoes and sprinkle with mozzarella cheese.

In a small bowl, mix together the breadcrumbs, oregano, and basil.

Season the breadcrumb mixture with salt and pepper to taste and sprinkle it over the top of the chicken.

Drizzle the chicken with olive oil.

Bake the chicken for 30 minutes, or until it is cooked through and the internal temperature reaches 165°F.

Serve the chicken hot, with your choice of sides.

Nutritional Information: Protein: 37g, Carbohydrate: 20g, Sugar: 5g, Sat Fat: 6g, Fiber: 2g,

Fat: 12g, Calories: 327

Beef And Vegetable Kebabs

Prep Time: 10 mins, **Servings:** 4, **Cooking Time:** 15 mins

Ingredients:

- 1 lb beef sirloin, cut into 1-inch cubes
- 1 bell pepper, cut into 1-inch pieces
- 1 onion, cut into 1-inch pieces
- 1 cup cherry tomatoes
- 1 tsp dried oregano
- 1 tsp dried basil
- Salt, to taste
- Pepper, to taste
- 4 skewers

Directions:

Preheat the grill to medium-high heat.

Thread the beef, bell pepper, onion, and cherry tomatoes onto the skewers, alternating the ingredients.

Season the kebabs with oregano, basil, salt, and pepper on all sides.

Grill the kebabs for 8-10 minutes, or until the beef is cooked to your desired level of doneness and the vegetables are tender.

Serve the kebabs hot, with your choice of sides.

Nutritional Information: Protein: 28g, Carbohydrate: 12g, Sugar: 7g, Sat Fat: 4g, Fiber: 2g, Fat: 12g, Calories: 238

Almond Butter Chicken

Prep Time: 10 mins, **Servings:** 4, **Cooking Time:** 20 mins

Ingredients:

- 4 chicken breasts
- 1/2 cup almond butter
- 1/4 cup honey
- 1/4 cup soy sauce
- 1 tsp grated ginger
- 1 clove garlic, minced
- Salt, to taste

- Pepper, to taste

Directions:

Preheat the oven to 350°F.

In a small bowl, whisk together the almond butter, honey, soy sauce, ginger, and garlic.

Place the chicken breasts in a baking dish and pour the almond butter mixture over the top.

Season the chicken with salt and pepper on both sides.

Bake the chicken for 20 minutes, or until it is cooked through and the internal temperature reaches 165°F.

Serve the chicken hot, with the pan juices spooned over the top.

Nutritional Information: Protein: 37g, Carbohydrate: 15g, Sugar: 13g, Sat Fat: 4g, Fiber: 1g, Fat: 15g, Calories

Chapter 3: Fish and Seafood Recipes

Mediterranean Baked Fish

Prep Time: 10mins, **Servings:** 4, **Cooking Time:** 20mins

Ingredients
- 1 pound of white fish fillets (such as cod or halibut)
- 1 cup of cherry tomatoes, halved
- 1/2 cup of pitted olives
- 1/4 cup of red onion, diced
- 2 tablespoons of olive oil
- 2 cloves of garlic, minced
- 1 teaspoon of dried oregano
- 1/2 teaspoon of dried basil
- 1/4 teaspoon of salt
- 1/4 teaspoon of black pepper
- 1 lemon, sliced into wedges

Directions
Preheat oven to 400°F. Place fish fillets in a baking dish.
In a small bowl, mix together cherry tomatoes, olives, red onion, olive oil, garlic, oregano, basil, salt, and pepper.

Spread the tomato mixture over the top of the fish fillets.
Bake for 20 minutes or until the fish is cooked through.
Serve with lemon wedges on the side.

Nutritional Information: Protein: 27g, Carbohydrate: 8g, Sugar: 3g, Sat Fat: 2g, Fiber: 2g, Fat: 12g, Calories: 214

Olive Turkey Patties

Prep Time: 10 mins, **Servings:** 4, **Cooking Time:** 20 mins

Ingredients:
- 1 lb ground turkey
- 1 egg
- 1 cup panko breadcrumbs
- 1 cup finely chopped green olives
- 1 tsp dried oregano
- 1 tsp dried basil
- 1 tsp garlic powder
- Salt, to taste
- Pepper, to taste
- 1 tbsp olive oil

Directions:
In a large bowl, mix together the ground turkey, egg, breadcrumbs, olives, oregano, basil, and garlic powder.
Season with salt and pepper to taste and mix until well combined.
Form the mixture into 4 patties.
In a large skillet, heat the olive oil over medium heat.
Add the patties to the skillet and cook for 5 minutes on each side, or until they are cooked through and browned on the outside.
Serve the patties hot, with your choice of toppings and sides.

Nutritional Information: Protein: 27g, Carbohydrate: 21g, Sugar: 2g, Sat Fat: 4g, Fiber: 2g, Fat: 13g, Calories: 267

Orzo, Bean, And Tuna Salad

Prep Time: 10 mins, **Servings:** 4, **Cooking Time:** 10 mins

Ingredients:
- 1 cup orzo
- 1 can kidney beans, drained and rinsed
- 1 can tuna, drained
- 1 cup cherry tomatoes, halved
- 1 small red onion, finely chopped

- ¼ cup chopped parsley
- ¼ cup olive oil
- 2 tbsp red wine vinegar
- 1 tsp Dijon mustard
- Salt, to taste
- Pepper, to taste

Directions:

In a large pot of boiling salted water, cook the orzo according to the package instructions.

Drain the orzo and transfer it to a large bowl.

Add the kidney beans, tuna, cherry tomatoes, red onion, and parsley to the bowl with the orzo.

In a small bowl, whisk together the olive oil, red wine vinegar, and Dijon mustard.

Pour the dressing over the orzo mixture and toss to combine.

Season with salt and pepper to taste and serve.

Nutritional Information: Protein: 17g, Carbohydrate: 46g, Sugar: 3g, Sat Fat: 4g, Fiber: 7g, Fat: 14g, Calories: 323

Catfish with Egg Pecans

Prep Time: 10mins, **Servings:** 4, **Cooking Time:** 20mins

Ingredients
- 1 pound of catfish fillets
- 1/2 cup of all-purpose flour
- 1/2 teaspoon of salt
- 1/4 teaspoon of black pepper
- 2 eggs, beaten
- 1/2 cup of pecans, finely chopped
- 1/4 cup of vegetable oil
- 1/4 cup of butter

Directions

In a shallow dish, mix together the flour, salt, and pepper. Dip the catfish fillets in the beaten eggs, then coat with the flour mixture.

In a large skillet, heat the oil and butter over medium-high heat. Add the catfish fillets and cook for 4-5 minutes on each side or until they are golden brown and cooked through.

Sprinkle the pecans over the top of the catfish fillets and serve.

Nutritional Information: Protein: 26g, Carbohydrate: 12g, Sugar: 1g, Sat Fat: 9g, Fiber: 2g, Fat: 27g, Calories: 358

Creamy Tuna Salad

Prep Time: 10mins, **Servings:** 4, **Cooking Time:** 0mins

Ingredients
- 2 cans of tuna, drained
- 1/2 cup of mayonnaise
- 1/4 cup of diced red onion
- 1/4 cup of diced celery
- 2 tablespoons of diced dill pickles
- 1 tablespoon of diced fresh parsley
- 1/2 teaspoon of lemon juice
- 1/4 teaspoon of salt
- 1/4 teaspoon of black pepper

Directions
In a medium bowl, mix together the tuna, mayonnaise, red onion, celery, dill pickles, parsley, lemon juice, salt, and pepper.
Serve the tuna salad on top of lettuce leaves or on bread as a sandwich.

Nutritional Information: Protein: 20g, Carbohydrate: 3g, Sugar: 2g, Sat Fat: 3g, Fiber: 1g, Fat: 15g, Calories: 191

Rosemary-Lemon Salmon

Prep Time: 10 mins, **Servings:** 4, **Cooking Time:** 15-20 mins

Ingredients
- 1 pound salmon fillets
- 1 lemon, juiced
- 1 tablespoon chopped fresh rosemary
- 1 tablespoon olive oil
- Salt and pepper, to taste

Directions
Preheat the oven to 375°F. Place the salmon fillets in a baking dish.
In a small bowl, mix together the lemon juice, rosemary, olive oil, salt, and pepper. Pour the mixture over the salmon.
Bake for 15-20 minutes, or until the salmon is cooked through and flakes easily with a fork.

Nutritional Information (per serving): Protein: 22g, Carbohydrates: 1g, Sugar: 0g, Sat Fat: 3g, Fiber: 0g, Fat: 6g, Calories: 139

Roast Salmon with Tarragon

Prep Time: 10 mins, **Servings:** 4, **Cooking Time:** 20-25 mins

Ingredients
- 1 pound salmon fillets
- 1 tablespoon olive oil
- 1 teaspoon chopped fresh tarragon
- 1 lemon, zested and juiced
- Salt and pepper, to taste

Directions
Preheat the oven to 400°F. Place the salmon fillets in a baking dish.

In a small bowl, mix together the olive oil, tarragon, lemon zest, lemon juice, salt, and pepper. Pour the mixture over the salmon.

Roast for 20-25 minutes, or until the salmon is cooked through and flakes easily with a fork.

Nutritional Information (per serving): Protein: 22g, Carbohydrates: 1g, Sugar: 0g, Sat Fat: 3g, Fiber: 0g, Fat: 6g, Calories: 139

Citrus Tilapia

Prep Time: 10 mins, **Servings:** 4, **Cooking Time:** 10-15 mins

Ingredients
- 1 pound tilapia fillets
- 1 orange, zested and juiced
- 1 lemon, zested and juiced
- 1 tablespoon olive oil
- 1 teaspoon chopped fresh parsley
- Salt and pepper, to taste

Directions

Heat a large skillet over medium heat. Add the olive oil and tilapia fillets.

In a small bowl, mix together the orange zest, orange juice, lemon zest, lemon juice, parsley, salt, and pepper. Pour the mixture over the tilapia.

Cook for 10-15 minutes, or until the tilapia is cooked through and flakes easily with a fork.

Nutritional Information (per serving): Protein: 22g, Carbohydrates: 3g, Sugar: 2g, Sat Fat: 2g, Fiber: 0g, Fat: 4g, Calories: 135

Crispy Trout with Herb

Prep Time: 15 mins, **Servings:** 2, **Cooking Time:** 15 mins

Ingredients:
- 1 large trout fillet, skin on
- 1 tbsp olive oil

- 1 tbsp butter
- 1 tsp chopped fresh herbs (such as parsley, dill, or chives)
- Salt and pepper, to taste

Directions:
Preheat the oven to 400°F.
Place the trout fillet, skin side down, on a lightly oiled baking sheet.
Brush the top of the trout with olive oil and sprinkle with the herbs, salt, and pepper.
Place a small pat of butter on top of each fillet.
Bake for 10-12 minutes, or until the fish is cooked through and the skin is crispy.
Serve the trout hot, garnished with additional herbs if desired.

Nutritional Information: Protein: 23g, Carbohydrates: 1g, Sugar: 0g, Sat Fat: 7g, Fiber: 0g, Fat: 13g, Calories: 213

Pasta with Lemon Spiced Shrimp and Cheese

Prep Time: 10 mins, **Servings:** 4, **Cooking Time:** 20 mins

Ingredients:
- 8 oz pasta of your choice
- 1 tbsp olive oil
- 1 lb large shrimp, peeled and deveined
- 1 tsp paprika
- 1 tsp garlic powder
- 1 tsp onion powder
- 1 tsp lemon zest
- 1 cup cherry tomatoes, halved
- 1 cup shredded cheese (such as mozzarella or cheddar)
- 1 tbsp chopped fresh basil

Directions:
Cook the pasta according to the package instructions. Drain and set aside.
In a large skillet, heat the olive oil over medium heat. Add the shrimp and cook for 2-3 minutes on each side, or until pink and cooked through.
Add the paprika, garlic powder, onion powder, and lemon zest to the skillet with the shrimp and stir to coat.
Add the cherry tomatoes and cooked pasta to the skillet and toss to combine.
Sprinkle the shredded cheese on top of the pasta mixture and place the skillet under the broiler for 2-3 minutes, or until the cheese is melted and bubbly.
Serve the pasta hot, garnished with chopped basil.

Nutritional Information: Protein: 37g, Carbohydrates: 51g, Sugar: 4g, Sat Fat: 10g, Fiber: 3g, Fat: 12g, Calories: 434

Za'atar Cod Fillets

Prep Time: 5 mins, **Servings:** 4, **Cooking Time:** 15 mins

Ingredients:
- 4 cod fillets
- 1 tbsp za'atar spice blend
- 1 tbsp olive oil
- Lemon wedges, for serving

Directions:
Preheat the oven to 400°F.
Place the cod fillets on a lightly oiled baking sheet.
Brush the fillets with olive oil and sprinkle with the za'atar spice blend.
Bake for 10-12 minutes, or until the fish is cooked through and flakes easily with a fork.
Serve the cod hot, garnished with lemon wedges.

Nutritional Information: Protein: 29g, Carbohydrates: 2g, Sugar: 0g, Sat Fat: 3g, Fiber: 0g, Fat: 5g, Calories: 171

Spicy Shrimp

Prep Time: 10mins, **Servings:** 4, **Cooking Time:** 10mins

Ingredients
- 1 pound large shrimp, peeled and deveined
- 1 tablespoon olive oil
- 1 teaspoon paprika
- 1 teaspoon cumin
- 1 teaspoon chili powder
- 1 teaspoon garlic powder
- 1/2 teaspoon salt
- 1/4 teaspoon black pepper

Directions
In a small bowl, mix together the paprika, cumin, chili powder, garlic powder, salt, and pepper.
Heat a large skillet over medium-high heat and add the olive oil.
Once the oil is hot, add the shrimp and sprinkle with the spice mixture.
Cook the shrimp for 2-3 minutes on each side, or until they are pink and cooked through.
Serve immediately.

Nutritional Information: Protein: 24g, Carbohydrate: 2g, Sugar: 0g, Sat Fat: 1.5g, Fiber: 0g, Fat: 5g, Calories: 152

Salmon Patties

Prep Time: 10mins, **Servings:** 4, **Cooking Time:** 10mins

Ingredients

- 1 (14.75 ounce) can pink salmon, drained and flaked
- 1 egg, beaten
- 1/4 cup bread crumbs
- 1/4 cup minced onion
- 1/4 cup minced celery
- 1 tablespoon minced fresh parsley
- 1/2 teaspoon salt
- 1/4 teaspoon ground black pepper
- 1 tablespoon olive oil

Directions

In a medium bowl, mix together the salmon, egg, bread crumbs, onion, celery, parsley, salt, and pepper.

Form the mixture into 4 patties.

Heat a large skillet over medium heat and add the olive oil.

Once the oil is hot, add the patties and cook for 4-5 minutes on each side, or until they are golden brown and cooked through.

Serve immediately.

Nutritional Information: Protein: 21g, Carbohydrate: 8g, Sugar: 1g, Sat Fat: 2g, Fiber: 1g, Fat: 10g, Calories: 182

Chapter 4: Vegetables & Side Dishes

Sautéed Spinach with Pumpkin Seeds

Prep Time: 5mins, **Servings:** 4, **Cooking Time:** 10mins

Ingredients

- 1 tablespoon of olive oil
- 1 clove of garlic, minced
- 1 pound of fresh spinach
- 1 tablespoon of pumpkin seeds
- Salt and pepper, to taste

Directions

Heat the olive oil in a large pan over medium heat. Add the garlic and cook until fragrant, about 1 minute.

Add the spinach to the pan and cook until wilted, about 3-4 minutes.

Sprinkle the pumpkin seeds over the spinach and season with salt and pepper.

Serve immediately.

Nutritional Information: Protein: 4g, Carbohydrate: 4g, Sugar: 0g, Sat Fat: 2g, Fiber: 2g, Fat: 7g, Calories: 90

Zucchini With Cheesy Lasagna

Prep Time: 10mins, **Servings:** 6, **Cooking Time:** 40mins

Ingredients

- 1 pound of ground beef
- 1 onion, diced
- 1 clove of garlic, minced
- 1 jar of marinara sauce
- 2 medium zucchini, thinly sliced lengthwise
- 1 cup of shredded mozzarella cheese
- 1 cup of ricotta cheese
- 1/2 cup of grated Parmesan cheese

Directions

Preheat the oven to 350°F.

In a large pan, cook the ground beef over medium heat until browned. Add the onion and garlic and cook until the onion is translucent. Stir in the marinara sauce.

Set aside.

Layer the zucchini slices in the bottom of a 9x13 inch baking dish.

Spread half of the meat mixture over the zucchini.

Top with half of the mozzarella cheese.

Repeat the layers, ending with the remaining mozzarella cheese.

Bake for 30-40 minutes, or until the zucchini is tender and the cheese is melted and bubbly.

Nutritional Information: Protein: 25g, Carbohydrate: 16g, Sugar: 10g, Sat Fat: 12g, Fiber: 4g, Fat: 25g, Calories: 350

Bean Curd Bake

Prep Time: 15mins, **Servings:** 4, **Cooking Time:** 45mins

Ingredients

- 1 package of firm bean curd, cut into 1 inch cubes
- 1 tablespoon of sesame oil
- 1 tablespoon of soy sauce
- 1 clove of garlic, minced
- 1 inch piece of ginger, grated
- 1 red bell pepper, diced
- 1 green bell pepper, diced
- 1 cup of broccoli florets
- 1 cup of sliced mushrooms
- 1 cup of diced tomatoes
- 1/2 cup of water

Directions

Preheat the oven to 375°F.

In a large bowl, toss the bean curd with the sesame oil, soy sauce, garlic, and ginger.

Spread the bean curd in a single layer on a baking sheet.

Bake for 15 minutes, or until the bean curd is browned and crispy.

In a large baking dish, combine the bell peppers, broccoli, mushrooms, and tomatoes.

Add the water and stir to combine.

Add the baked bean curd to the top of the vegetables.

Bake for 30 minutes, or until the vegetables are tender.

Nutritional Information: Protein: 15g, Carbohydrate: 20g, Sugar: 8g, Sat Fat: 4g, Fiber: 10g, Fat: 10g, Calories: 220

Spaghetti Squash with Walnuts and Parmesan

Prep Time: 15mins, **Servings:** 4, **Cooking Time:** 45mins

Ingredients

- 1 large spaghetti squash

- 2 tablespoons olive oil
- 1/2 cup chopped walnuts
- 1/2 cup grated parmesan cheese
- 2 cloves garlic, minced
- 1/4 cup chopped parsley
- Salt and pepper, to taste

Directions

Preheat the oven to 400 degrees Fahrenheit. Scoop out the seeds after cutting the spaghetti squash in half lengthwise.

Roast the squash halves, cut-side down, on a baking sheet for 40-45 minutes, or until soft.

Meanwhile, in a small saucepan over medium heat, heat the olive oil. Cook until the chopped walnuts are gently browned, about 5 minutes.

Remove the squash from the oven and scrape the spaghetti-like strands into a large mixing dish with a fork.

Toss the squash with the toasted walnuts, grated parmesan, minced garlic, and chopped parsley. To mix, toss everything together.

Season with salt and pepper to taste, and serve immediately.

Nutritional Information (per serving): Calories: 222, Fat: 18g, Saturated Fat: 4g, Cholesterol: 12mg, Sodium: 216mg, Carbohydrates: 14g, Fiber: 3g, Sugar: 5g, Protein: 9g

Celery With Mushroom Bolognese

Prep Time: 15mins, **Servings:** 4, **Cooking Time:** 45mins

Ingredients

- 1 pound ground beef
- 1 small onion, diced
- 8 ounces mushrooms, diced
- 1 celery stalk, diced
- 1 garlic clove, minced
- 1 (14.5-ounce) can diced tomatoes
- 1/2 cup red wine
- 1 teaspoon dried basil
- 1 teaspoon dried oregano
- 1/2 teaspoon salt
- 1/4 teaspoon black pepper
- 1/4 teaspoon red pepper flakes (optional)

- 4 celery stalks, cut into 1/2-inch slices
- 1/4 cup grated Parmesan cheese

Directions

Heat a large skillet over medium heat. Add the ground beef and cook until browned, breaking it up into small pieces as it cooks.

Add the onion, mushrooms, and diced celery to the pan and cook until the vegetables are softened, about 5-7 minutes.

Stir in the garlic and cook for an additional minute.

Add the canned tomatoes, red wine, basil, oregano, salt, black pepper, and red pepper flakes (if using). Bring the mixture to a simmer and cook for 10-15 minutes, or until the sauce has thickened.

Meanwhile, bring a pot of salted water to a boil. Add the celery slices and cook for 2-3 minutes, or until they are tender but still crisp.

Drain the celery and divide it among four plates. Top with the mushroom bolognese sauce and sprinkle with grated Parmesan cheese. Serve hot.

Nutritional Information (per serving): Calories: 259, Fat: 13g, Saturated Fat: 5g, Cholesterol: 53mg, Sodium: 468mg, Carbohydrates: 14g, Fiber: 3g, Sugar: 8g, Protein: 22g

Spicy Pear Tacos
Prep Time: 15mins, **Servings:** 4, **Cooking Time:** 15mins

Ingredients

- 1 tablespoon olive oil
- 1 medium onion, diced
- 1 jalapeno pepper, seeded and minced
- 2 cloves garlic, minced
- 2 ripe pears, cored and diced
- 1 teaspoon chili powder
- 1 teaspoon cumin
- 1/2 teaspoon salt
- 1/4 teaspoon black pepper
- 8 small corn tortillas
- 1/2 cup crumbled feta cheese
- 1/4 cup chopped fresh cilantro

Directions

Heat the olive oil in a large skillet over medium heat. Add the onion and jalapeno and cook until the onion is translucent, about 5 minutes.

Stir in the garlic and cook for an additional minute

Serving size: 2 tacos (1/4 of recipe): Calories: 214, Total fat: 9g, Saturated fat: 4g, Cholesterol: 23mg, Sodium: 402mg, Total carbohydrate: 30g, Dietary fiber: 4g, Sugar: 6g, Protein: 6g

Sesame Spinach

Prep Time: 10 mins, **Servings:** 4, **Cooking Time:** 5 mins

Ingredients

- 1 pound fresh spinach leaves
- 1 tablespoon sesame oil
- 1 tablespoon soy sauce
- 1 tablespoon honey
- 1 teaspoon sesame seeds

Directions

Wash the spinach leaves and pat dry with paper towels.

Heat the sesame oil in a large pan over medium heat.

Add the spinach to the pan and cook for 2-3 minutes, stirring occasionally, until the spinach is wilted.

In a small bowl, mix together the soy sauce, honey, and sesame seeds.

Pour the sauce over the spinach and stir to coat the spinach evenly.

Cook for an additional 2 minutes, until the sauce has thickened and the spinach is coated in the sauce.

Serve immediately, garnished with additional sesame seeds if desired.

Serving size: 1/4 of recipe: Calories: 54 Total fat: 3g, Saturated fat: 0g, Cholesterol: 0mg, Sodium: 365mg, Total carbohydrate: 6g, Dietary fiber: 1g, Sugar: 4g, Protein: 2g

Cheese Crepes With Spinach

Prep Time: 20 mins, **Servings:** 4, **Cooking Time:** 20 mins

Ingredients

- 1 cup all-purpose flour

- 2 eggs
- 1 cup milk
- 1/4 teaspoon salt
- 2 tablespoons butter, melted
- 1 cup shredded cheese
- 1 cup cooked and chopped spinach

Directions

In a medium bowl, whisk together the flour, eggs, milk, and salt until smooth.

Heat a small nonstick pan over medium heat. Brush with a small amount of melted butter.

Pour in a small amount of the crepe batter, enough to coat the bottom of the pan in a thin layer. Cook until the edges begin to curl and the bottom is lightly browned, about 1-2 minutes.

Flip the crepe and cook the other side for an additional 1-2 minutes. Repeat with remaining batter.

Place a small amount of cheese and cooked spinach in the center of each crepe. Fold the crepe in half and then in half again to form a triangle.

Heat a large pan over medium heat and add the filled crepes. Cook until the cheese is melted and the crepes are heated through, about 2-3 minutes per side.

Serve the crepes hot, garnished with additional cheese if desired.

Serving size: 1 crepe: Calories: 212, Total fat: 14g, Saturated fat: 8g, Cholesterol: 101mg, Sodium: 259mg, Total carbohydrate: 15g, Dietary fiber: 1g, Sugar: 3g, Protein: 9g

Vegetarian Gyros
Prep Time: 10mins, **Servings:** 4, **Cooking Time:** 15mins

Ingredients

- 1 medium eggplant, sliced into thin rounds
- 1 red bell pepper, sliced into thin strips
- 1 yellow bell pepper, sliced into thin strips
- 1 red onion, sliced into thin rounds
- 1 tablespoon olive oil
- 1 teaspoon cumin
- 1 teaspoon paprika
- 1 teaspoon garlic powder
- 1 teaspoon onion powder
- 1 teaspoon dried oregano
- 1 teaspoon dried basil

- 1 pinch of salt
- 4 pita breads
- 1 cup tzatziki sauce
- 1 cup shredded lettuce
- 1 cup diced tomatoes

Directions

Preheat a grill or grill pan to medium-high heat.

In a small bowl, mix together the cumin, paprika, garlic powder, onion powder, oregano, basil, and salt.

Brush the eggplant and bell peppers with olive oil and sprinkle with the spice mixture. Grill for about 7-8 minutes on each side, or until tender and slightly charred.

Grill the pita bread for about 1-2 minutes on each side, or until warmed and slightly crispy.

To assemble the gyros, spread some tzatziki sauce on each pita bread. Top with the grilled vegetables, lettuce, and tomatoes. Roll up the pita bread and serve.

Serving size: 1 gyro: Calories: 358, Total fat: 14g, Saturated fat: 2g, Cholesterol: 7mg, Sodium: 837mg, Total carbohydrate: 46g, Dietary fiber: 5g, Sugar: 10g, Protein: 11g

Umami Mushrooms

Prep Time: 5mins, **Servings:** 4, **Cooking Time:** 20mins

Ingredients

- 1 pound mixed mushrooms (such as shiitake, cremini, and portobello), sliced
- 1 tablespoon olive oil
- 1 tablespoon soy sauce
- 1 teaspoon balsamic vinegar
- 1 teaspoon Worcestershire sauce
- 1 teaspoon honey
- 1 clove garlic, minced
- 1 pinch of salt
- 1 pinch of black pepper

Directions

In a large pan, heat the olive oil over medium heat. Add the mushrooms and sauté for about 5-7 minutes, or until tender and slightly browned.

In a small bowl, whisk together the soy sauce, balsamic vinegar, Worcestershire sauce, honey, garlic, salt, and pepper. Pour the sauce over the mushrooms and stir to coat.

Reduce the heat to low and simmer for about 10-15 minutes, or until the sauce has thickened and the mushrooms are fully coated.

Serve the mushrooms over rice, quinoa, or noodles. Optional: sprinkle with some chopped green onions or sesame seeds for extra flavor.

Serving size: 1/4 of recipe: Calories: 71, Total fat: 4g, Saturated fat: 1g, Cholesterol: 0mg, Sodium: 402mg, Total carbohydrate: 8g, Dietary fiber: 2g, Sugar: 4g, Protein: 3g

Creamy Vegetable Quiche
Prep Time: 15mins, **Servings:** 6, **Cooking Time:** 45mins

Ingredients:

- 1 refrigerated pie crust
- 1 cup diced onions
- 1 cup diced bell peppers
- 1 cup diced mushrooms
- 1 cup diced broccoli
- 1 cup diced asparagus
- 3 large eggs
- 1 cup milk
- 1 cup heavy cream
- 1 cup grated cheddar cheese
- 1 teaspoon salt
- 1 teaspoon black pepper

Directions:

Preheat the oven to 375°F.

Press the pie crust into a 9-inch pie dish and prick the bottom with a fork.

In a large skillet, sauté the onions, bell peppers, mushrooms, broccoli, and asparagus until tender.

In a large mixing bowl, whisk together the eggs, milk, heavy cream, cheese, salt, and pepper.

Stir in the sautéed vegetables and pour the mixture into the pie crust.

Bake the quiche for 45 minutes or until it is set and the top is golden brown.

Allow the quiche to cool for 10 minutes before slicing and serving.

Nutritional Information (per serving): Protein: 11g, Carbohydrate: 17g, Sugar: 6g, Sat Fat: 10g, Fiber: 2g, Fat: 22g, Calories: 291

Lentils and Rice

Prep Time: 10mins, **Servings:** 4, **Cooking Time:** 45mins

Ingredients:

- 1 cup uncooked brown rice
- 1 cup uncooked lentils
- 2 cups water
- 1 tablespoon olive oil
- 1 medium onion, diced
- 2 cloves garlic, minced
- 1 teaspoon ground cumin
- 1 teaspoon ground coriander
- 1 teaspoon ground turmeric
- 1 teaspoon ground paprika
- 1/2 teaspoon salt
- 1/4 teaspoon black pepper
- 1 cup diced tomatoes
- 1 cup vegetable broth
- 1 cup frozen peas
- 1/2 cup chopped fresh cilantro

Directions:

Rinse the rice and lentils and add them to a medium saucepan with the water. Bring the mixture to a boil, then reduce the heat to a simmer and cover the pan. Cook for 45 minutes or until the rice and lentils are tender.

In a separate large skillet, heat the olive oil over medium heat. Add the onions and garlic and sauté until the onions are translucent.

Add the cumin, coriander, turmeric, paprika, salt, and pepper to the skillet and stir to combine.

Stir in the tomatoes, vegetable broth, peas, and cooked rice and lentils. Bring the mixture to a boil, then reduce the heat to a simmer and cook for an additional 10 minutes.

Stir in the cilantro and serve the lentils and rice hot.

Nutritional Information (per serving): Protein: 10g, Carbohydrate: 37g, Sugar: 5g, Sat Fat: 1g, Fiber: 11g, Fat: 2g, Calories: 216

Cauliflower Mashed "Potatoes"

Prep Time: 10mins, **Servings:** 4, **Cooking Time:** 15mins

Ingredients

- 1 large head of cauliflower, cut into florets
- 2 cloves garlic, minced
- 2 tablespoons unsalted butter
- 1/4 cup milk
- 1/4 cup grated Parmesan cheese
- Salt and pepper, to taste

Directions

Bring a large pot of salted water to a boil. Add the cauliflower florets and cook until tender, about 10 minutes.

Drain the cauliflower and transfer to a blender or food processor. Add the garlic, butter, milk, Parmesan cheese, salt, and pepper. Blend until smooth and creamy.

Transfer the mashed cauliflower to a serving bowl and serve hot.

Serving size: 1/4 of recipe: Calories: 105, Total fat: 8g, Saturated fat: 5g, Cholesterol: 24mg, Sodium: 201mg, Total carbohydrate: 7g, Dietary fiber: 3g, Sugar: 3g, Protein: 5g

Cannellini Bean Pizza

Prep Time: 10mins, **Servings:** 4, **Cooking Time:** 15mins

Ingredients

- 1 pre-made pizza crust
- 1/2 cup canned cannellini beans, drained and rinsed
- 1/4 cup tomato sauce
- 1/4 cup grated mozzarella cheese
- 1/4 cup diced cherry tomatoes
- 1/4 cup diced red onion
- 1 tablespoon olive oil
- 1 tablespoon chopped fresh basil
- Salt and pepper, to taste

Directions

Preheat the oven to 425°F (220°C).

Place the pizza crust on a baking sheet. Spread the cannellini beans and tomato sauce over the crust. Sprinkle with the mozzarella cheese, cherry tomatoes, and red onion. Drizzle with olive oil and sprinkle with basil, salt, and pepper.

Bake the pizza for 10-15 minutes, or until the crust is golden brown and the cheese is melted.

Serve hot and enjoy!

Serving size: 1/4 of recipe: Calories: 301, Total fat: 11g, Saturated fat: 3g, Cholesterol: 10mg, Sodium: 627mg, Total carbohydrate: 41g, Dietary fiber: 6g, Sugar: 3g, Protein: 10g

Vegetable Fruit Bowl with Lentil

Prep Time: 15 mins, **Servings:** 4, **Cooking Time:** 20 mins

Ingredients:

- 1 cup dried green lentils
- 2 cups water
- 1/2 teaspoon salt
- 1 cup diced vegetables (such as bell peppers, cucumber, and cherry tomatoes)
- 1 cup diced fruit (such as mango, pineapple, and kiwi)
- 1/4 cup chopped fresh herbs (such as parsley, basil, and cilantro)
- 1/4 cup crumbled feta cheese

For the dressing:

- 2 tablespoons olive oil
- 2 tablespoons red wine vinegar
- 1 clove garlic, minced
- 1/2 teaspoon salt
- 1/4 teaspoon black pepper

Directions:

In a small saucepan, bring the lentils, water, and salt to a boil. Reduce the heat to a simmer and cook until the lentils are tender, about 15-20 minutes.

In a small bowl, whisk together the olive oil, red wine vinegar, garlic, salt, and pepper.

In a large bowl, combine the cooked lentils, diced vegetables, diced fruit, and chopped herbs. Drizzle with the dressing and toss to coat.

Top the bowl with crumbled feta cheese and serve. Enjoy!

Nutritional Information: Protein: 13g, Carbohydrate: 35g, Sugar: 8g, Sat Fat: 3g, Fiber: 14g, Fat: 8g, Calories: 267

Healthy Banana Cookies With Oatmeal

Prep Time: 10 mins, **Servings:** 24, **Cooking Time:** 15 mins

Ingredients:

- 2 ripe bananas, mashed
- 1 cup quick oats
- 1/2 cup almond butter
- 1/4 cup honey
- 1 egg
- 1 teaspoon vanilla extract
- 1/2 teaspoon baking soda
- 1/2 teaspoon salt
- 1/2 cup dark chocolate chips (optional)

Directions:

Preheat the oven to 3500F. Line a baking sheet with parchment paper.

In a large bowl, mash the bananas using a fork or potato masher.

Add the oats, almond butter, honey, egg, vanilla extract, baking soda, and salt to the bowl with the mashed bananas. Mix until well combined.

Stir in the chocolate chips, if using.

Drop the dough by the tablespoonful onto the prepared baking sheet.

Bake the cookies for 12-15 minutes, or until they are golden brown.

Allow the cookies to cool on the baking sheet for a few minutes before transferring them to a wire rack to cool completely. Serve and enjoy!

Nutritional Information: Protein: 5g, Carbohydrate: 18g, Sugar: 10g, Sat Fat: 3g, Fiber: 2g, Fat: 8g, Calories: 141

Fried Rice Tom Yum

Prep Time: 10 mins, **Servings:** 4, **Cooking Time:** 15 mins

Ingredients:

- 2 cups cooked white rice

- 1 tablespoon vegetable oil
- 1/2 cup diced chicken
- 1/2 cup diced shrimp
- 1/2 cup diced vegetables (such as bell peppers, onions, and carrots)
- 1/4 cup tom yum paste
- 1/4 cup chicken broth
- 1 tablespoon fish sauce
- 1 tablespoon lime juice
- 1/4 cup chopped fresh cilantro

Directions:

Heat the vegetable oil in a large pan over medium heat.

Add the chicken, shrimp, and vegetables to the pan and cook until they are just cooked through, about 5 minutes.

Add the tom yum paste, chicken broth, fish sauce, and lime juice to the pan and stir to combine.

Add the cooked rice to the pan and stir to coat with the tom yum mixture.

Cook for an additional 2-3 minutes, or until the rice is heated through.

Garnish with chopped cilantro and serve hot. Enjoy!

Nutritional Information: Protein: 23g, Carbohydrate: 49g, Sugar: 4g, Sat Fat: 4g, Fiber: 2g, Fat: 7g, Calories: 311

Fried Legume

Prep Time: 10 mins, **Servings:** 4, **Cooking Time:** 15 mins

Ingredients:

- 1 cup dried legumes (such as lentils, chickpeas, or black beans)
- 4 cups water
- 1 tablespoon vegetable oil
- 1/2 cup diced vegetables (such as bell peppers, onions, and carrots)
- 1/2 cup diced tomatoes

- 1/2 cup diced onions
- 1 clove garlic, minced
- 1 teaspoon chili powder
- 1/2 teaspoon cumin
- 1/2 teaspoon salt
- 1/4 cup chopped fresh cilantro

Directions:

In a large saucepan, bring the legumes and water to a boil. Reduce the heat to a simmer and cook until the legumes are tender, about 30-45 minutes.

Heat the vegetable oil in a large pan over medium heat.

Add the vegetables, tomatoes, onions, and garlic to the pan and cook until they are tender, about 5-7 minutes.

Add the chili powder, cumin, and salt to the pan and stir to combine.

Drain the cooked legumes and add them to the pan with the vegetables. Stir to coat with the seasoning.

Cook for an additional 2-3 minutes, or until the legumes are heated through.

Garnish with chopped cilantro and serve hot. Enjoy!

Nutritional Information: Protein: 14g, Carbohydrate: 37g, Sugar: 6g, Sat Fat: 2g, Fiber: 12g, Fat: 4g, Calories: 240

Slow Cooker Quinoa Lentil Tacos

Prep Time: 15 mins, **Servings:** 4, **Cooking Time:** 4 hours

Ingredients

- 1 cup quinoa, rinsed
- 1 cup brown lentils, rinsed
- 2 cups vegetable broth
- 1 cup salsa
- 1 tsp cumin

- 1 tsp chili powder
- 1 tsp garlic powder
- 1 tsp onion powder
- Salt, to taste
- 1 cup chopped bell peppers
- 1 cup chopped onions
- 1 cup chopped tomatoes
- 8 corn tortillas
- Optional toppings: avocado, cilantro, cheese, sour cream

Directions

In a slow cooker, combine quinoa, lentils, broth, salsa, cumin, chili powder, garlic powder, onion powder, and salt. Stir to combine.

Add bell peppers, onions, and tomatoes to the slow cooker and stir to combine.

Cover the slow cooker and cook on low for 4 hours, or until quinoa and lentils are cooked and tender.

Heat corn tortillas in a dry pan over medium heat until warmed and slightly crispy.

To assemble the tacos, spoon quinoa lentil mixture into the corn tortillas and top with optional toppings as desired.

Serving size: 2 tacos (1/4 of recipe): Calories: 337, Total fat: 5g, Saturated fat: 1g, Cholesterol: 0mg, Sodium: 962mg, Total carbohydrate: 60g, Dietary fiber: 17g, Sugar: 5g, Protein: 16g

Butter Bean Penne

Prep Time: 10 mins, **Servings:** 4, **Cooking Time:** 20 mins

Ingredients

- 1 package (16 oz) penne pasta
- 2 tbsp olive oil
- 1 small onion, diced
- 3 cloves garlic, minced
- 1 can (14.5 oz) diced tomatoes
- 1 can (15 oz) butter beans, drained and rinsed
- 1 cup vegetable broth
- 1 tsp Italian seasoning
- 1/4 tsp salt
- 1/4 tsp black pepper
- 1/4 cup chopped fresh parsley

Directions

Cook the penne pasta according to package instructions.

In a large pan, heat the olive oil over medium heat. Add the onion and garlic and cook until the onion is translucent, about 5 minutes.

Add the diced tomatoes, butter beans, broth, Italian seasoning, salt, and pepper to the pan. Bring to a simmer and cook for 5 minutes.

Add the cooked and drained penne pasta to the pan and stir to combine.

Serve the pasta topped with fresh parsley. Optional: top with grated Parmesan cheese.

Serving size: 1/4 of recipe: Calories: 429. Total fat: 10g, Saturated fat: 1g, Cholesterol: 0mg, Sodium: 682mg, Total carbohydrate: 73g, Dietary fiber: 7g, Sugar: 6g, Protein: 15g

Chapter 5: Soup Recipes

Healthy Bean Soup

Prep Time: 15mins, **Servings:** 4, **Cooking Time:** 45mins

Ingredients

- 1 cup of mixed beans (such as kidney beans, black beans, and pinto beans)
- 1 cup of chopped vegetables (such as carrots, onions, and bell peppers)
- 1 clove of minced garlic
- 1 teaspoon of olive oil
- 4 cups of low-sodium vegetable broth
- 1 teaspoon of cumin
- 1 teaspoon of chili powder
- Salt and pepper, to taste

Directions

In a large pot, heat the olive oil over medium heat. Add the garlic and vegetables and cook for 5 minutes, until the vegetables are tender.

Add the mixed beans, vegetable broth, cumin, and chili powder to the pot. Bring to a boil, then reduce the heat to a simmer.

Simmer for 30 minutes, or until the beans are tender.

Season with salt and pepper, to taste.

Serving size: 1/4 of recipe: Calories: 122, Total fat: 2g, Saturated fat: 0g, Cholesterol: 0mg, Sodium: 976mg, Total carbohydrate: 22g, Dietary fiber: 7g, Sugar: 3g, Protein: 6g

Veggie Pea Soup

Prep Time: 10mins, **Servings:** 4, **Cooking Time:** 30mins

Ingredients

- 1 tablespoon of olive oil
- 1 cup of chopped onions
- 1 cup of chopped carrots
- 1 cup of chopped celery
- 1 clove of minced garlic
- 1 cup of frozen peas
- 4 cups of low-sodium vegetable broth
- 1 teaspoon of thyme
- Salt and pepper, to taste

Directions

In a large pot, heat the olive oil over medium heat. Add the onions, carrots, celery, and garlic and cook for 5 minutes, until the vegetables are tender.

Add the peas, vegetable broth, and thyme to the pot. Bring to a boil, then reduce the heat to a simmer.

Simmer for 20 minutes, or until the vegetables are tender.

Season with salt and pepper, to taste. Serve hot.

Serving size: 1 cup: Calories: 84 Total Fat: 3g Saturated Fat: 0.5g Trans Fat: 0g Cholesterol: 0mg Sodium: 254mg Total Carbohydrates: 13g Dietary Fiber: 3g Sugars: 6g Protein: 3g Vitamin A: 65% Vitamin C: 17% Calcium: 2% Iron: 4%

Flavors Corn Soup

Prep Time: 20mins, **Servings:** 4, **Cooking Time:** 30mins

Ingredients

- 1 tbsp olive oil

- 1 small onion, diced
- 1 small red bell pepper, diced
- 1 small yellow bell pepper, diced
- 1 small jalapeno pepper, seeded and minced
- 1 clove garlic, minced
- 1 tsp ground cumin
- 1 tsp chili powder
- 1 cup frozen corn
- 4 cups vegetable broth
- 1 can (14.5 oz) diced tomatoes
- 1/2 cup uncooked quinoa
- 1/4 cup chopped fresh cilantro

Directions

In a large pot, heat the oil over medium heat. Add the onion, bell peppers, jalapeno pepper, and garlic. Cook until the vegetables are tender, about 5 minutes.

Stir in the cumin and chili powder. Add the corn, broth, and tomatoes. Bring to a boil.

Reduce the heat to low and simmer for 15 minutes.

Stir in the quinoa and continue to simmer until the quinoa is cooked, about 10 minutes.

Stir in the cilantro and serve hot.

Nutritional Information: Protein: 7g, Carbohydrates: 23g, Sugar: 8g, Sat Fat: 1g, Fiber: 3g, Fat: 5g, Calories: 152

Fruit & Veg Soup

Prep Time: 10mins, **Servings:** 4, **Cooking Time:** 20mins

Ingredients

- 1 tbsp olive oil
- 1 small onion, diced
- 1 clove garlic, minced
- 1 medium carrot, peeled and diced
- 1 medium potato, peeled and diced
- 1 small zucchini, diced
- 1 cup frozen mixed vegetables

- 4 cups vegetable broth
- 1 can (14.5 oz) diced tomatoes
- 1/2 cup frozen mixed fruit
- 1/4 cup chopped fresh parsley

Directions

In a large pot, heat the oil over medium heat. Add the onion and garlic. Cook until the onion is translucent, about 5 minutes.

Add the carrot, potato, zucchini, and mixed vegetables. Cook for an additional 5 minutes.

Add the broth and tomatoes. Bring to a boil.

Reduce the heat to low and simmer for 10 minutes.

Stir in the frozen mixed fruit and continue to simmer until the fruit is thawed and the vegetables are tender, about 5 minutes.

Stir in the parsley and serve hot.

Nutritional Information: Protein: 5g, Carbohydrates: 25g, Sugar: 14g, Sat Fat: 1g, Fiber: 4g, Fat: 4g, Calories: 150

Tomato Tofu Soup

Prep Time: 15mins, **Servings:** 4, **Cooking Time:** 30mins

Ingredients

- 1 tablespoon olive oil
- 1 medium onion, diced
- 2 cloves garlic, minced
- 1 (14.5 oz) can diced tomatoes
- 4 cups vegetable broth
- 1 (14 oz) block firm tofu, drained and cubed
- 1 teaspoon dried basil
- 1 teaspoon dried oregano
- 1 teaspoon dried thyme
- 1 teaspoon salt
- 1/2 teaspoon black pepper

Directions

In a large pot, heat the olive oil over medium heat. Add the diced onion and minced garlic, and cook until the onion is translucent.

Add the diced tomatoes, vegetable broth, cubed tofu, basil, oregano, thyme, salt, and black pepper to the pot. Bring the mixture to a boil, then reduce the heat to low and simmer for 20 minutes.

Use an immersion blender to blend the soup until it reaches your desired consistency. Alternatively, you can transfer the soup to a blender and blend it in batches.

Serve the soup hot, garnished with some fresh herbs or a sprinkle of cheese if desired.

Nutritional Information (per serving): Protein: 11g, Carbohydrates: 20g, Sugar: 8g, Sat Fat: 1g, Fiber: 4g, Fat: 5g, Calories: 146

Potato Squash Soup

Prep Time: 15mins, **Servings:** 4, **Cooking Time:** 45mins

Ingredients

- 1 tablespoon olive oil
- 1 medium onion, diced
- 2 cloves garlic, minced
- 1 small butternut squash, peeled and diced
- 3 medium potatoes, peeled and diced
- 4 cups vegetable broth
- 1 teaspoon dried rosemary
- 1 teaspoon dried thyme
- 1 teaspoon salt
- 1/2 teaspoon black pepper
- 1/2 cup milk (optional)

Directions

In a large pot, heat the olive oil over medium heat. Add the diced onion and minced garlic, and cook until the onion is translucent.

Add the diced squash and potatoes, vegetable broth, rosemary, thyme, salt, and black pepper to the pot. Bring the mixture to a boil, then reduce the heat to low and simmer for 30 minutes or until the vegetables are tender.

Use an immersion blender to blend the soup until it reaches your desired consistency. Alternatively, you can transfer the soup to a blender and blend it in batches.

Stir in the milk (if using) and heat through. Serve the soup hot, garnished with some fresh herbs or a sprinkle of cheese if desired.

Nutritional Information (per serving): Protein: 6g, Carbohydrates: 36g, Sugar: 8g, Sat Fat: 1g, Fiber: 6g, Fat: 3g, Calories: 214

Silky Zucchini Soup

Prep Time: 15mins, **Servings:** 4, **Cooking Time:** 30mins

Ingredients

- 1 tablespoon olive oil
- 1 medium onion, diced
- 2 cloves garlic, minced
- 4 medium zucchini, diced
- 4 cups vegetable broth
- 1 cup coconut milk
- 1 teaspoon dried basil
- 1 teaspoon dried oregano
- 1 teaspoon salt
- 1/2 teaspoon black pepper

Directions

In a large pot, heat the olive oil over medium heat. Add the diced onion and minced garlic, and cook until the onion is translucent.

Add the diced zucchini, vegetable broth, coconut milk, basil, oregano, salt, and black pepper to the pot. Bring the mixture to a boil, then reduce the heat to low and simmer for 20 minutes or until the zucchini is tender.

Use an immersion blender to blend the soup until it reaches your desired consistency. Alternatively, you can transfer the soup to a blender and blend it in batches.

Serve the soup hot, garnished with some fresh herbs or a sprinkle of cheese if desired.

Nutritional Information (per serving): Protein: 5g, Carbohydrates: 13g, Sugar: 10g, Sat Fat: 7g, Fiber: 2g, Fat: 17g, Calories: 229

Spicy Bean Soup

Prep Time: 15mins, **Servings:** 4, **Cooking Time:** 45mins

Ingredients

- 1 tablespoon olive oil
- 1 medium onion, diced
- 2 cloves garlic, minced
- 1 jalapeno pepper, seeded and diced
- 1 (15 oz) can kidney beans, drained and rinsed
- 1 (14.5 oz) can diced tomatoes
- 4 cups vegetable broth
- 1 teaspoon ground cumin
- 1 teaspoon chili powder
- 1 teaspoon salt
- 1/2 teaspoon black pepper
- 1 cup cooked brown rice (optional)

Directions

In a large pot, heat the olive oil over medium heat. Add the diced onion, minced garlic, and jalapeno pepper, and cook until the onion is translucent.

Add the kidney beans, diced tomatoes, vegetable broth, cumin, chili powder, salt, and black pepper to the pot. Bring the mixture to a boil, then reduce the heat to low and simmer for 30 minutes.

Use an immersion blender to blend the soup until it reaches your desired consistency. Alternatively, you can transfer the soup to a blender and blend it in batches.

Stir in the cooked brown rice (if using) and heat through. Serve the soup hot, garnished with some fresh herbs or a sprinkle of cheese if desired.

Nutritional Information (per serving without rice): Protein: 8g, Carbohydrates: 22g, Sugar: 6g, Sat Fat: 1g, Fiber: 8g, Fat: 3g, Calories: 141

Nutritional Information (per serving with rice): Protein: 10g, Carbohydrates: 35g, Sugar: 6g, Sat Fat: 1g, Fiber: 8g, Fat: 3g, Calories: 216

Flavors Vegetable Stew

Prep Time: 15mins, **Servings:** 4, **Cooking Time:** 1 hour

Ingredients

- 1 tablespoon olive oil
- 1 medium onion, diced
- 2 cloves garlic, minced

- 1 large carrot, peeled and diced
- 1 large sweet potato, peeled and diced
- 1 large bell pepper, diced
- 1 cup frozen peas
- 1 (14.5 oz) can diced tomatoes
- 4 cups vegetable broth
- 1 teaspoon dried basil
- 1 teaspoon dried oregano
- 1 teaspoon dried thyme
- 1 teaspoon salt
- 1/2 teaspoon black pepper

Directions

In a large pot, heat the olive oil over medium heat. Add the diced onion and minced garlic, and cook until the onion is translucent.

Add the diced carrot, sweet potato, bell pepper, frozen peas, diced tomatoes, vegetable broth, basil, oregano, thyme, salt, and black pepper to the pot. Bring the mixture to a boil, then reduce the heat to low and simmer for 45 minutes or until the vegetables are tender.

Serve the stew hot, garnished with some fresh herbs or a sprinkle of cheese if desired.

Nutritional Information (per serving): Protein: 6g, Carbohydrates: 28g, Sugar: 10g, Sat Fat: 1g, Fiber: 8g, Fat: 3g, Calories: 170

Butternut Soup

Prep Time: 15mins, **Servings:** 4, **Cooking Time:** 45mins

Ingredients

- 1 tablespoon olive oil
- 1 medium onion, diced
- 2 cloves garlic, minced
- 1 large butternut squash, peeled and diced
- 4 cups vegetable broth
- 1 cup coconut milk
- 1 teaspoon dried basil
- 1 teaspoon dried oregano
- 1 teaspoon salt
- 1/2 teaspoon black pepper

Directions

In a large pot, heat the olive oil over medium heat. Add the diced onion and minced garlic, and cook until the onion is translucent.

Add the diced butternut squash, vegetable broth, coconut milk, basil, oregano, salt, and black pepper to the pot. Bring the mixture to a boil, then reduce the heat to low and simmer for 30 minutes or until the squash is tender.

Use an immersion blender to blend the soup until it reaches your desired consistency. Alternatively, you can transfer the soup to a blender and blend it in batches.

Serve the soup hot, garnished with some fresh herbs or a sprinkle of cheese if desired.

Nutritional Information (per serving): Protein: 5g, Carbohydrates: 18g, Sugar: 8g, Sat Fat: 7g, Fiber: 4g, Fat: 15g, Calories: 217

Lentil Veggie Stew

Prep Time: 15mins, **Servings:** 4, **Cooking Time:** 1 hour

Ingredients

- 1 tablespoon olive oil
- 1 medium onion, diced
- 2 cloves garlic, minced
- 1 cup green lentils, rinsed
- 1 large carrot, peeled and diced
- 1 large sweet potato, peeled and diced
- 1 large bell pepper, diced
- 1 cup frozen peas
- 1 (14.5 oz) can diced tomatoes
- 4 cups vegetable broth
- 1 teaspoon dried basil
- 1 teaspoon dried oregano
- 1 teaspoon dried thyme
- 1 teaspoon salt
- 1/2 teaspoon black pepper

Directions

In a large pot, heat the olive oil over medium heat. Add the diced onion and minced garlic, and cook until the onion is translucent.

Add the green lentils, diced carrot, sweet potato, bell pepper, frozen peas, diced tomatoes, vegetable broth, basil, oregano, thyme, salt, and black pepper to the pot. Bring the mixture to a boil, then reduce the heat to low and simmer for 45 minutes or until the vegetables and lentils are tender.

Serve the stew hot, garnished with some fresh herbs or a sprinkle of cheese if desired.

Nutritional Information (per serving): Protein: 11g, Carbohydrates: 35g, Sugar: 10g, Sat Fat: 1g, Fiber: 12g, Fat: 3g, Calories: 214

Homestyle Bean Soup

Prep Time: 15mins, **Servings:** 4, **Cooking Time:** 45mins

Ingredients

- 1 tablespoon olive oil
- 1 medium onion, diced
- 2 cloves garlic, minced
- 1 (15 oz) can kidney beans, drained and rinsed
- 1 (15 oz) can navy beans, drained and rinsed
- 1 (14.5 oz) can diced tomatoes
- 4 cups vegetable broth
- 1 teaspoon dried basil
- 1 teaspoon dried oregano
- 1 teaspoon salt
- 1/2 teaspoon black pepper
- 1 cup cooked brown rice (optional)

Directions

In a large pot, heat the olive oil over medium heat. Add the diced onion and minced garlic, and cook until the onion is translucent.

Add the kidney beans, navy beans, diced tomatoes, vegetable broth, basil, oregano, salt, and black pepper to the pot. Bring the mixture to a boil, then reduce the heat to low and simmer for 30 minutes.

Stir in the cooked brown rice (if using) and heat through. Serve the soup hot, garnished with some fresh herbs or a sprinkle of cheese if desired.

Nutritional Information (per serving without rice): Protein: 13g, Carbohydrates: 32g, Sugar: 6g, Sat Fat: 1g, Fiber: 12g, Fat: 3g, Calories: 190

Nutritional Information (per serving with rice): Protein: 15g, Carbohydrates: 45g, Sugar: 6g, Sat Fat: 1g, Fiber: 12g, Fat: 3g, Calories: 265

Chapter 6: Snack Recipes

Berry Greek Yogurt Parfaits with Granola

Prep Time: 10mins, **Servings:** 4

Ingredients

- 2 cups Greek yogurt
- 1 cup mixed berries (such as strawberries, blueberries, and raspberries)
- 1 cup granola

Directions

In four small glasses or bowls, divide the Greek yogurt evenly.

Top each serving of yogurt with a quarter of the mixed berries.

Sprinkle granola over the top of the berries.

Repeat the layers of yogurt, berries, and granola until all ingredients are used up.

Serve the parfaits immediately, or cover and refrigerate until ready to serve.

Nutritional Information (per serving): Protein: 16g, Carbohydrates: 38g, Sugar: 22g, Sat Fat: 1g, Fiber: 4g, Fat: 6g, Calories: 260

Hummus

Prep Time: 15mins, **Servings:** 4

Ingredients

- 1 (15 oz) can chickpeas, drained and rinsed
- 3 tablespoons tahini
- 3 tablespoons lemon juice
- 2 cloves garlic, minced
- 1/4 teaspoon salt
- 1/4 teaspoon cumin
- 3 tablespoons water

Directions

Place the chickpeas, tahini, lemon juice, garlic, salt, and cumin in a food processor or blender.

Process the mixture until it is smooth, adding water as needed to achieve a creamy consistency.

Serve the hummus immediately, or transfer it to a covered container and refrigerate until ready to serve.

Nutritional Information (per serving): Protein: 6g, Carbohydrates: 9g, Sugar: 1g, Sat Fat: 2g, Fiber: 3g, Fat: 5g, Calories: 101

Lentil Trail Mix

Prep Time: 20mins, **Servings:** 4

Ingredients

- 1 cup dried lentils
- 1 cup mixed nuts (almonds, cashews, peanuts)
- 1 cup dried fruit (raisins, cranberries, apricots)
- 1 tsp paprika
- 1 tsp cumin
- 1 tsp chili powder

Directions

Rinse and drain the lentils, then add them to a pot with 2 cups of water. Bring to a boil, then reduce the heat and simmer for 20 minutes or until tender.

Drain any excess water from the lentils and allow them to cool.

In a large mixing bowl, combine the cooled lentils, mixed nuts, and dried fruit.

In a small bowl, mix together the paprika, cumin, and chili powder. Sprinkle the spice mixture over the trail mix and stir to coat evenly.

Serve the trail mix as a snack or pack it in a container to take on-the-go.

Serving size: 1/2 cup: Calories: 214 Total Fat: 9g Saturated Fat: 1g Trans Fat: 0g Cholesterol: 0mg Sodium: 7mg Total Carbohydrates: 28g Dietary Fiber: 7g Sugars: 9g Protein: 8g Vitamin A: 4% Vitamin C: 0% Calcium: 4% Iron: 14%

Thyme Mushrooms

Prep Time: 5 mins, **Servings:** 4, **Cooking Time:** 10 mins

Ingredients

- 1 pound button mushrooms, cleaned and sliced
- 2 tbsp butter
- 1 tbsp thyme leaves
- 1 tbsp minced garlic
- Salt and pepper, to taste

Directions

In a large skillet, melt the butter over medium-high heat.

Add the sliced mushrooms and cook for 5-7 minutes, stirring occasionally, until they are tender and browned.

Add the thyme, garlic, salt, and pepper to the skillet and stir to combine.

Continue cooking for an additional 2-3 minutes, or until the garlic is fragrant.

Serve the thyme mushrooms as a side dish or add them to pasta, rice, or a salad.

Serving size: 1/4 of the recipe: Calories: 91 Total Fat: 8g Saturated Fat: 5g Trans Fat: 0g Cholesterol: 20mg Sodium: 146mg Total Carbohydrates: 5g Dietary Fiber: 2g Sugars: 3g Protein: 3g Vitamin A: 2% Vitamin C: 4% Calcium: 2% Iron: 4%

Honey-Lime Berry Salad

Prep Time: 10 mins, **Servings:** 4, **Cooking Time:** 0 mins

Ingredients

- 4 cups mixed berries (strawberries, raspberries, blueberries)
- 3 tbsp honey
- 2 tbsp lime juice
- 1 cup chopped fresh mint leaves

Directions

In a large mixing bowl, combine the mixed berries, honey, and lime juice. Stir gently to coat the berries in the honey and lime juice.

Add the chopped mint leaves to the bowl and toss to combine.

Serve the berry salad as a side dish or a refreshing dessert.

Serving size: 1 cup: Calories: 110 Total Fat: 0g Saturated Fat: 0g Trans Fat: 0g Cholesterol: 0mg Sodium: 1mg Total Carbohydrates: 29g Dietary Fiber: 4g Sugars: 22g Protein: 1g Vitamin A: 6% Vitamin C: 80% Calcium: 2% Iron: 2%

Pickled Cucumbers

Prep Time: 10 mins, **Servings:** 4, **Cooking Time:** 10 mins

Ingredients

- 1 pound small cucumbers, thinly sliced
- 1 cup water
- 1 cup white vinegar
- 1 tbsp sugar
- 1 tsp salt
- 1 tsp mustard seeds
- 1 tsp dill seeds

Directions

In a small saucepan, bring the water, vinegar, sugar, and salt to a boil. Stir to dissolve the sugar and salt.

Place the sliced cucumbers in a clean jar or container with a tight-fitting lid.

Add the mustard seeds and dill seeds to the jar with the cucumbers.

Pour the hot vinegar mixture over the cucumbers, making sure to completely cover them.

Allow the pickled cucumbers to cool to room temperature, then seal the jar and refrigerate for at least 4 hours or overnight.

Serve the pickled cucumbers as a side dish or use them to add flavor to sandwiches and salads.

Serving size: 1/4 of the recipe: Calories: 19 Total Fat: 0g Saturated Fat: 0g Trans Fat: 0g Cholesterol: 0mg Sodium: 557mg Total Carbohydrates: 5g Dietary Fiber: 0g Sugars: 4g Protein: 0g Vitamin A: 0% Vitamin C: 2% Calcium: 0% Iron: 0%

Nutritious Roasted Chickpeas

Prep Time: 5 mins, **Servings:** 4, **Cooking Time:** 35 mins

Ingredients

- 1 can chickpeas, drained and rinsed
- 1 tbsp olive oil
- 1 tsp paprika
- 1 tsp cumin
- 1 tsp garlic powder
- Salt and pepper, to taste

Directions

Preheat the oven to 400°F.

In a small bowl, mix together the paprika, cumin, garlic powder, salt, and pepper.

In a large mixing bowl, toss the chickpeas in the olive oil until they are evenly coated.

Sprinkle the spice mixture over the chickpeas and toss to coat evenly.

Spread the seasoned chickpeas in a single layer on a baking sheet.

Roast the chickpeas for 35 minutes, or until they are crispy and golden brown.

Serve the roasted chickpeas as a snack or add them to salads and grain bowls for added protein.

Whipped Ricotta Toast

Prep Time: 5 mins, **Servings:** 4, **Cooking Time:** 0 mins

Ingredients

- 1 cup ricotta cheese
- 1 tbsp honey
- 1 tsp vanilla extract
- 4 slices bread (such as sourdough or baguette)
- 1 cup mixed berries

Directions

In a small mixing bowl, use a fork to mash together the ricotta cheese, honey, and vanilla extract until smooth and creamy.

Toast the bread slices until they are lightly golden.

Spread the whipped ricotta mixture evenly over the toast slices.

Top the toast with the mixed berries.

Serve the whipped ricotta toast as a breakfast or snack.

Brussel Sprouts Hummus

Prep Time: 10 mins, **Servings:** 4, **Cooking Time:** 20 mins

Ingredients

- 1 pound brussels sprouts, trimmed and halved
- 2 cloves garlic
- 1 can chickpeas, drained and rinsed
- 2 tbsp tahini
- 1 tbsp lemon juice
- 1 tsp cumin
- Salt and pepper, to taste

Directions

Preheat the oven to 400°F.

On a baking sheet, toss the brussels sprouts with a drizzle of olive oil and a pinch of salt. Roast for 20 minutes, or until they are tender and caramelized.

In a food processor, combine the roasted brussels sprouts, garlic, chickpeas, tahini, lemon juice, cumin, salt, and pepper. Blend until smooth and creamy.

Serve the brussel sprouts hummus with crackers, vegetables, or pita bread.

Curried Cannellini Bean Dip

Prep Time: 5 mins, **Servings:** 4, **Cooking Time:** 0 mins

Ingredients

- 1 can cannellini beans, drained and rinsed
- 1 tbsp curry powder
- 1 tbsp lemon juice
- 2 cloves garlic, minced
- 1 tbsp olive oil
- Salt and pepper, to taste

Directions

In a food processor, combine the cannellini beans, curry powder, lemon juice, garlic, olive oil, salt, and pepper. Blend until smooth and creamy.

Serve the curried cannellini bean dip with crackers, vegetables, or pita bread. You can also use it as a spread for sandwiches or wraps.

Sikil Peak (Pumpkin Seed Salsa)

Prep Time: 10 mins, **Servings:** 4, **Cooking Time:** 0 mins

Ingredients

- 1 cup pumpkin seeds, toasted
- 1 cup diced tomatoes
- 1 cup diced red onion
- 1 jalapeno pepper, seeded and diced
- 1/4 cup chopped fresh cilantro
- 2 tbsp lime juice
- 1 tsp ground cumin
- Salt and pepper, to taste

Directions

In a food processor, pulse the pumpkin seeds until they are finely ground.

In a large mixing bowl, combine the ground pumpkin seeds, diced tomatoes, diced red onion, diced jalapeno pepper, chopped cilantro, lime juice, cumin, salt, and pepper. Stir to combine.

Serve the pumpkin seed salsa with tortilla chips, vegetables, or as a topping for tacos or burritos.

Cottage Cheese Mousse

Prep Time: 5 mins, **Servings:** 4, **Cooking Time:** 0 mins

Ingredients

- 1 cup cottage cheese
- 1/2 cup heavy cream
- 1 tsp vanilla extract
- 1 tsp honey

Directions

In a food processor, blend the cottage cheese, heavy cream, vanilla extract, and honey until smooth and creamy.

Serve the cottage cheese mousse as a dessert or a protein-rich snack. You can also add it to breakfast bowls or use it as a topping for toast or fruit.

Oat Nuggets

Prep Time: 10 mins, **Servings:** 4, **Cooking Time:** 15 mins

Ingredients

- 1 cup rolled oats
- 1/2 cup ground flaxseeds
- 1/2 cup almond flour
- 1 tsp baking powder
- 1 tsp ground cinnamon
- 1/2 tsp salt
- 1 egg
- 1/2 cup almond milk
- 1/4 cup honey

Directions

Preheat the oven to 350°F. Line a baking sheet with parchment paper.

In a large mixing bowl, combine the rolled oats, ground flaxseeds, almond flour, baking powder, cinnamon, and salt. Stir to combine.

In a separate mixing bowl, whisk together the egg, almond milk, and honey.

Pour the wet mixture into the dry mixture and stir until everything is well combined.

Drop spoonfuls of the oat mixture onto the prepared baking sheet, forming small nuggets.

Bake the oat nuggets for 15 minutes, or until they are golden brown and crispy.

Serve the oat nuggets as a snack or breakfast treat.

Crispy Carrot Fries

Prep Time: 5 mins, **Servings:** 4, **Cooking Time:** 20 mins

Ingredients

- 1 pound carrots, cut into thin fries
- 2 tbsp olive oil
- 1 tsp garlic powder
- 1 tsp paprika
- 1 tsp dried oregano
- Salt and pepper, to taste

Directions

Preheat the oven to 400°F. Line a baking sheet with parchment paper.

In a large mixing bowl, toss the carrots in the olive oil until they are evenly coated.

In a small bowl, mix together the garlic powder, paprika, oregano, salt, and pepper. Sprinkle the spice mixture over the carrots and toss to coat evenly.

Spread the seasoned carrots in a single layer on the prepared baking sheet.

Bake the carrot fries for 20 minutes, or until they are tender and crispy.

Serve the carrot fries as a side dish or snack.

Sweet Potato Hummus

Prep Time: 10 mins, **Servings:** 4, **Cooking Time:** 40 mins

Ingredients

- 1 medium sweet potato, peeled and diced
- 1 can chickpeas, drained and rinsed
- 2 tbsp tahini
- 1 tbsp lemon juice
- 1 tsp cumin
- 1/4 tsp salt
- 1/4 tsp pepper
- 1/4 cup water

Directions

Preheat the oven to 400°F.

On a baking sheet, toss the diced sweet potato with a drizzle of olive oil and a pinch of salt. Roast for 40 minutes, or until they are tender and caramelized.

In a food processor, combine the roasted sweet potato, chickpeas, tahini, lemon juice, cumin, salt, pepper, and water. Blend until smooth and creamy.

Serve the sweet potato hummus with crackers, vegetables, or pita bread.

Lime Wild Rice

Prep Time: 10 mins, **Servings:** 4, **Cooking Time:** 45 mins

Ingredients

- 1 cup wild rice
- 2 cups water
- 1 tsp salt
- 1 tbsp olive oil
- 1 clove garlic, minced
- 1 tbsp lime juice
- 1 tsp ground cumin
- 1/4 cup chopped fresh cilantro

Directions

In a medium saucepan, bring the wild rice, water, and salt to a boil. Reduce the heat to low and simmer, covered, for 45 minutes, or until the rice is tender and the water is absorbed.

In a small skillet, heat the olive oil over medium heat. Add the garlic and cook for 1-2 minutes, or until fragrant.

Stir in the lime juice and cumin.

Add the cooked wild rice to the skillet and toss to coat with

Cannellini Bean Hummus

Prep Time: 10 mins, **Servings:** 4, **Cooking Time:** 0 mins

Ingredients

- 1 can cannellini beans, drained and rinsed
- 2 cloves garlic
- 2 tbsp tahini
- 1 tbsp lemon juice
- 1 tsp cumin
- Salt and pepper, to taste

Directions

In a food processor, combine the cannellini beans, garlic, tahini, lemon juice, cumin, salt, and pepper. Blend until smooth and creamy.

Serve the cannellini bean hummus with crackers, vegetables, or pita bread.

Spiced Chickpeas With Peppered Parsley

Prep Time: 5 mins, **Servings:** 4, **Cooking Time:** 15 mins

Ingredients

- 1 can chickpeas, drained and rinsed
- 1 tbsp olive oil
- 1 tsp paprika
- 1 tsp cumin
- 1 tsp garlic powder
- 1/4 tsp salt
- 1/4 tsp black pepper
- 1/4 cup chopped fresh parsley

Directions

Preheat the oven to 400°F.

On a baking sheet, toss the chickpeas in the olive oil until they are evenly coated.

In a small bowl, mix together the paprika, cumin, garlic powder, salt, and black pepper. Sprinkle the spice mixture over the chickpeas and toss to coat evenly.

Spread the seasoned chickpeas in a single layer on the baking sheet.

Bake the chickpeas for 15 minutes, or until they are crispy and golden brown.

Sprinkle the chopped parsley over the spiced chickpeas before serving. Enjoy as a snack or add them to salads and grain bowls for added protein.

Avocado Tomato Salsa

Prep Time: 10mins, **Servings:** 4, **Cooking Time:** 0mins

Ingredients

- 1 avocado, diced
- 1 tomato, diced
- 1 small onion, diced
- 1 jalapeno pepper, diced
- 1 clove garlic, minced
- 1 lime, juiced
- 1 handful fresh cilantro, chopped
- Salt, to taste

Directions

Combine all ingredients in a medium bowl. Mix well to combine. Serve immediately, or refrigerate until ready to serve. Enjoy with chips, on top of grilled chicken or fish, or as a topping for tacos or burritos.

Nutritional Information: Protein: 2g, Carbohydrate: 12g, Sugar: 3g, Sat Fat: 0.5g, Fiber: 6g, Fat: 10g, Calories: 123

Lemon Brussels Sprouts

Prep Time: 10mins, **Servings:** 4, **Cooking Time:** 20mins

Ingredients

- 1 pound Brussels sprouts, trimmed and halved
- 1 tablespoon olive oil
- 1 lemon, zested and juiced
- Salt and pepper, to taste

Directions

Preheat the oven to 400°F. Line a baking sheet with parchment paper.

In a large bowl, toss the Brussels sprouts with the olive oil, lemon zest, lemon juice, salt, and pepper. Spread the Brussels sprouts out on the prepared baking sheet in a single layer.

Roast the Brussels sprouts for 20 minutes, or until tender and browned. Serve hot, garnished with additional lemon zest and juice, if desired.

Nutritional Information: Protein: 4g, Carbohydrate: 14g, Sugar: 4g, Sat Fat: 1g, Fiber: 4g, Fat: 7g, Calories: 126

Chapter 7: Desserts Recipes

Watermelon Berry Ice Pops

Prep Time: 10 mins, **Servings:** 6, **Cooking Time:** 0 mins

Ingredients

- 2 cups cubed watermelon

- 1 cup mixed berries (such as strawberries, raspberries, and blueberries)
- 1/2 cup coconut water
- 2 tbsp honey

Directions

In a blender, combine the watermelon, mixed berries, coconut water, and honey. Blend until smooth.

Pour the watermelon berry mixture into ice pop molds, leaving a little bit of space at the top for expansion.

Freeze the ice pops for at least 4 hours, or until solid.

To remove the ice pops from the molds, run the molds under warm water for a few seconds.

Serve the watermelon berry ice pops as a refreshing summer treat.

Apricot Crisp

Prep Time: 10 mins, **Servings:** 4, **Cooking Time:** 30 mins

Ingredients

- 4 cups apricots, pitted and sliced
- 1/4 cup all-purpose flour
- 1/4 cup brown sugar
- 1/2 cup old-fashioned oats
- 1/4 cup butter, melted
- 1 tsp ground cinnamon

Directions

Preheat the oven to 350°F.

In a large mixing bowl, toss the sliced apricots with the flour.

Spread the apricots in an even layer in a baking dish.

Baked Apples With Almonds

Prep Time: 10 mins, **Servings:** 4, **Cooking Time:** 30 mins

Ingredients

- 4 large apples, cored and sliced

- 1/2 cup chopped almonds
- 1/4 cup honey
- 1 tsp ground cinnamon
- 1 tsp vanilla extract

Directions

Preheat the oven to 350°F.

In a small mixing bowl, combine the chopped almonds, honey, cinnamon, and vanilla extract.

Arrange the sliced apples in a single layer in a baking dish.

Top the apples with the almond mixture.

Bake the apples for 30 minutes, or until they are tender and caramelized.

Serve the baked apples with a scoop of vanilla ice cream or a drizzle of cream.

Berries Crumble

Prep Time: 10 mins, **Servings:** 4, **Cooking Time:** 30 mins

Ingredients

- 2 cups mixed berries (such as strawberries, raspberries, and blueberries)
- 1/2 cup all-purpose flour
- 1/2 cup old-fashioned oats
- 1/2 cup brown sugar
- 1/4 cup butter, melted
- 1 tsp ground cinnamon

Directions

Preheat the oven to 350°F.

In a large mixing bowl, toss the mixed berries with 1/4 cup of the flour.

Spread the berry mixture in an even layer in a baking dish.

In a separate mixing bowl, combine the remaining 1/4 cup of flour, oats, brown sugar, melted butter, and cinnamon. Stir until everything is well combined.

Sprinkle the oat mixture over the top of the berries.

Bake the berry crumble for 30 minutes, or until the top is crispy and the berries are bubbly.

Serve the berry crumble warm, with a scoop of vanilla ice cream or a drizzle of cream.

Honeydew Balsamic Glaze

Prep Time: 10 mins, **Servings:** 4, **Cooking Time:** 15 mins

Ingredients

- 1 small honeydew, peeled and cubed
- 1/4 cup balsamic vinegar
- 1 tbsp honey
- 1 tsp cornstarch
- 1 tsp water

Directions

In a small saucepan, combine the honeydew, balsamic vinegar, and honey. Bring to a boil over medium heat.

In a small bowl, mix together the cornstarch and water to form a slurry. Add the slurry to the honeydew mixture, stirring until the glaze thickens.

Remove the glaze from the heat and let it cool slightly.

Serve the honeydew balsamic glaze over grilled chicken or pork, or as a dipping sauce for grilled vegetables.

Chocolate Mousse

Prep Time: 10 mins, **Servings:** 4, **Cooking Time:** 0 mins

Ingredients

- 1 cup heavy cream
- 1/2 cup semisweet chocolate chips
- 1 tsp vanilla extract
- 1 tbsp sugar

Directions

In a medium saucepan, heat the heavy cream until it is hot but not boiling.

Add the chocolate chips to the hot cream and let them sit for a few minutes to soften.

Stir the chocolate chips until they are fully melted and the mixture is smooth.

Add the vanilla extract and sugar to the chocolate mixture, stirring until everything is well combined.

Let the chocolate mousse cool to room temperature, then refrigerate it for at least 2 hours, or until it is set.

Serve the chocolate mousse in small bowls or glasses, topped with whipped cream and a sprinkle of cocoa powder.

Refreshing Watermelon Ice Pops

Prep Time: 10 mins, **Servings:** 6, **Cooking Time:** 0 mins

Ingredients

- 2 cups cubed watermelon
- 1/4 cup coconut water
- 1 tbsp honey
- 1 tsp lime juice

Directions

In a blender, combine the watermelon, coconut water, honey, and lime juice. Blend until smooth.

Pour the watermelon mixture into ice pop molds, leaving a little bit of space at the top for expansion.

Freeze the ice pops for at least 4 hours, or until solid.

To remove the ice pops from the molds, run the molds under warm water for a few seconds.

Serve the watermelon ice pops as a refreshing summer treat.

Berries With Balsamic Vinegar

Prep Time: 10 mins, **Servings:** 4, **Cooking Time:** 0 mins

Ingredients

- 2 cups mixed berries (such as strawberries, raspberries, and blueberries)
- 1/4 cup balsamic vinegar
- 1 tbsp honey

Directions

In a small mixing bowl, combine the balsamic vinegar and honey.

In a separate bowl, toss the mixed berries with the balsamic vinegar mixture.

Serve the berries with a drizzle of the balsamic vinegar mixture, or store the berries in the refrigerator until ready to serve.

The berry mixture can be served as a topping for yogurt or ice cream, or as a side dish with grilled chicken or pork.

Cookie Cream Shake

Prep Time: 10 mins, **Servings:** 2, **Cooking Time:** 0 mins

Ingredients

- 1 cup milk
- 1/2 cup vanilla ice cream
- 1/4 cup crumbled chocolate chip cookies
- 1 tbsp chocolate syrup

Directions

In a blender, combine the milk, ice cream, chocolate chip cookies, and chocolate syrup. Blend until smooth.

Pour the shake into two glasses and serve immediately.

The shake can be garnished with whipped cream and additional crumbled chocolate chip cookies, if desired.

Strawberry Mint Yogurt

Prep Time: 10 mins, **Servings:** 4, **Cooking Time:** 0 mins

Ingredients

- 2 cups Greek yogurt
- 1 cup chopped strawberries
- 1/4 cup chopped fresh mint
- 1 tbsp honey

Directions

In a medium mixing bowl, combine the Greek yogurt, chopped strawberries, chopped mint, and honey. Stir until everything is well combined.

Serve the strawberry mint yogurt in small bowls or glasses, topped with additional chopped strawberries and mint.

The yogurt can also be served as a topping for waffles or pancakes, or as a dip for fruit.

Banana Pecan Muffins

Prep Time: 10 mins, **Servings:** 12, **Cooking Time:** 20 mins

Ingredients

- 1 cup all-purpose flour
- 1 tsp baking powder
- 1/2 tsp baking soda
- 1/4 tsp salt
- 1/4 cup butter, melted
- 1/2 cup brown sugar
- 1 egg
- 1 cup mashed bananas
- 1/4 cup milk
- 1/2 cup pecans, chopped

Directions

Preheat the oven to 350°F (180°C). Grease a muffin tin or line with muffin cups.

In a medium mixing bowl, whisk together the flour, baking powder, baking soda, and salt.

In a separate mixing bowl, beat together the melted butter and brown sugar until well combined. Beat in the egg, mashed bananas, and milk until smooth.

Add the wet mixture to the dry mixture and stir until just combined. Fold in the chopped pecans.

Divide the batter evenly among the muffin cups, filling each cup about 3/4 full.

Bake the muffins for 18-20 minutes, or until a toothpick inserted into the center of a muffin comes out clean.

Allow the muffins to cool in the tin for a few minutes before transferring them to a wire rack to cool completely.

Baked Apple Slices

Prep Time: 10 mins, **Servings:** 4, **Cooking Time:** 15 mins

Ingredients

- 4 apples, cored and sliced
- 1/4 cup butter, melted

- 1/4 cup brown sugar
- 1 tsp cinnamon

Directions

Preheat the oven to 350°F (180°C). Grease a baking dish.

Arrange the sliced apples in the prepared baking dish.

In a small mixing bowl, whisk together the melted butter, brown sugar, and cinnamon. Pour the mixture over the apples.

Bake the apples for 15 minutes, or until tender.

Serve the baked apple slices as a side dish or topping for ice cream.

Creamy Delicious Farro

Prep Time: 10 mins, **Servings:** 4, **Cooking Time:** 45 mins

Ingredients

- 1 cup farro
- 2 cups water
- 1/4 tsp salt
- 1 cup milk
- 1/4 cup heavy cream
- 1/4 cup grated Parmesan cheese
- 1/4 tsp nutmeg
- 1/4 tsp black pepper
- 1/4 cup chopped parsley

Directions

In a medium saucepan, bring the water and salt to a boil. Add the farro and reduce the heat to low. Simmer for about 45 minutes, or until the farro is tender.

Drain any excess water from the farro and return it to the saucepan. Add the milk, heavy cream, Parmesan cheese, nutmeg, and black pepper. Stir until the cheese is melted and the mixture is creamy.

Stir in the chopped parsley and serve the farro hot.

Creamy Fruit Dessert

Prep Time: 10 mins, **Servings:** 4, **Cooking Time:** 5 mins

Ingredients

- 2 cups mixed fruit (such as strawberries, bananas, and grapes)
- 1/2 cup vanilla yogurt
- 1/4 cup whipped cream
- 1/4 cup granola

Directions

Wash and chop the mixed fruit into bite-size pieces.

In a medium mixing bowl, stir together the vanilla yogurt and whipped cream until smooth.

Divide the mixed fruit among four bowls or glasses. Top each bowl with a spoonful of the creamy mixture and a sprinkle of granola.

Serve the creamy fruit dessert chilled or at room temperature.

Black Bean Bars

Prep Time: 10 mins, **Servings:** 16, **Cooking Time:** 20 mins

Ingredients

- 1 1/2 cups black beans, rinsed and drained
- 1 cup quick oats
- 1/2 cup all-purpose flour
- 1/2 cup unsweetened cocoa powder
- 1/2 cup brown sugar
- 1/2 cup vegetable oil
- 2 eggs
- 1 tsp vanilla extract
- 1 tsp baking powder
- 1/2 tsp salt
- 1/2 cup chocolate chips

Directions

Preheat the oven to 350°F. Grease an 8-inch square baking pan.

In a food processor, pulse the black beans, oats, flour, cocoa powder, brown sugar, vegetable oil, eggs, vanilla extract, baking powder, and salt until smooth. Stir in the chocolate chips.

Pour the mixture into the prepared pan and smooth the top. Bake for 20 minutes, or until the bars are set and a toothpick inserted in the center comes out clean.

Let the bars cool in the pan for a few minutes before cutting into squares and serving.

Cheddar Cake

Prep Time: 10 mins, **Servings:** 8, **Cooking Time:** 45 mins

Ingredients

- 1 cup all-purpose flour
- 1 cup grated cheddar cheese
- 1/2 cup butter, melted
- 1/2 cup milk
- 1/2 cup sugar
- 2 eggs
- 1 tsp baking powder
- 1/2 tsp salt

Directions

Preheat the oven to 350°F. Grease a 9-inch round cake pan.

In a medium mixing bowl, stir together the flour, cheddar cheese, melted butter, milk, sugar, eggs,

Brown Rice Pudding

Prep Time: 15mins, **Servings:** 4, **Cooking Time:** 45mins

Ingredients

- 1 cup uncooked brown rice
- 2 cups water
- 1 cinnamon stick
- 1 cup milk
- 1 cup heavy cream
- 1/2 cup sugar
- 1 tsp vanilla extract
- 1/4 tsp salt
- 1/4 tsp ground cinnamon

Directions

Rinse the brown rice in cold water and add it to a medium saucepan with the water and cinnamon stick. Bring the mixture to a boil, reduce the heat to low, and simmer, covered, for 45 minutes, or until the rice is tender and the water is absorbed.

In a separate saucepan, combine the milk, cream, sugar, vanilla extract, salt, and ground cinnamon. Cook over medium heat, stirring constantly, until the sugar has dissolved.

Add the cooked rice to the milk mixture and stir to combine. Cook over low heat for an additional 5-10 minutes, or until the pudding has thickened and is heated through.

Serve the pudding warm or chilled, garnished with a sprinkle of cinnamon if desired.

Nutritional Information: Protein: 4g, Carbohydrate: 50g, Sugar: 30g, Sat Fat: 8g, Fiber: 2g, Fat: 15g, Calories: 358

Yogurt Cheesecake

Prep Time: 30mins, **Servings:** 8, **Cooking Time:** 1hr

Ingredients

- 1 1/2 cups graham cracker crumbs
- 1/4 cup butter, melted
- 2 cups plain Greek yogurt
- 1 cup granulated sugar
- 3 tablespoons all-purpose flour
- 3 large eggs
- 1 teaspoon vanilla extract
- 1/4 teaspoon salt

Directions

Preheat the oven to 350°F and grease a 9-inch springform pan.

In a medium bowl, mix together the graham cracker crumbs and melted butter until well combined. Press the mixture into the bottom of the prepared pan and set aside.

In a large bowl, beat the yogurt, sugar, flour, eggs, vanilla extract, and salt until well combined. Pour the mixture over the graham cracker crust in the pan.

Bake the cheesecake for 50-60 minutes, or until the center is set and the edges are lightly golden brown.

Allow the cheesecake to cool completely before slicing and serving.

Nutritional Information: Protein: 10g, Carbohydrate: 42g, Sugar: 27g, Sat Fat: 7g, Fiber: 1g, Fat: 18g, Calories: 337

Banana Cream Nonfat Yogurt

Prep Time: 5 mins, **Servings:** 1, **Cooking Time:** 0 mins

Ingredients:

- 1 small banana, sliced
- 1 cup nonfat vanilla yogurt
- 2 tbsp honey
- 1 tsp vanilla extract

Directions:

In a blender, combine the banana, yogurt, honey, and vanilla extract.

Blend until smooth and creamy.

Pour into a bowl or glass and serve immediately.

Nutritional Information: Protein: 8g, Carbohydrate: 41g, Sugar: 32g, Sat Fat: 0g, Fiber: 2g, Fat: 0g, Calories: 178

Pistachio-Stuffed Dates

Prep Time: 10 mins, **Servings:** 6, **Cooking Time:** 0 mins

Ingredients:

- 12 pitted dates
- 6 tsp unsalted pistachios, finely chopped
- 6 tsp cream cheese

Directions:

Slice each date lengthwise and remove the pit.

Fill each date with 1 tsp of cream cheese and 1 tsp of chopped pistachios.

Close the date and press gently to secure the filling.

Repeat with the remaining dates and serve immediately.

Nutritional Information: Protein: 3g, Carbohydrate: 26g, Sugar: 21g, Sat Fat: 3g, Fiber: 3g, Fat: 5g, Calories: 148

Meringues With Strawberries, Mint, And Toasted Coconut

Prep Time: 15 mins, **Servings:** 4, **Cooking Time:** 1 hr 15 mins

Ingredients:

3 egg whites

¾ cup sugar

1 tsp vanilla extract

1 cup strawberries, sliced

1 tbsp fresh mint, finely chopped

¼ cup coconut flakes, toasted

Directions:

Preheat the oven to 200°F and line a baking sheet with parchment paper.

In a large mixing bowl, beat the egg whites until stiff peaks form.

Gradually add the sugar, 1 tbsp at a time, beating constantly until the mixture is stiff and glossy.

Stir in the vanilla extract.

Drop the mixture by spoonfuls onto the prepared baking sheet, leaving about 2 inches between each one.

Bake for 1 hour and 15 minutes, or until the meringues are crisp on the outside and dry to the touch.

Let the meringues cool on the baking sheet for 5 minutes before transferring to a wire rack to cool completely.

Just before serving, top the meringues with sliced strawberries, chopped mint, and toasted coconut.

Nutritional Information: Protein: 3g, Carbohydrate: 45g, Sugar: 44g, Sat Fat: 0g, Fiber: 1g, Fat: 0g, Calories: 186

Baked Pear Crisp

Prep Time: 10 mins, **Servings:** 6, **Cooking Time:** 45 mins

Ingredients:

- Filling:
- 3 large pears, peeled and sliced

- 1 tbsp lemon juice
- 1 tbsp sugar
- 1 tsp cinnamon

Topping:

- 1 cup old-fashioned oats
- ¼ cup all-purpose flour
- ¼ cup brown sugar
- 1 tsp cinnamon
- 6 tbsp unsalted butter, melted

Directions:

Preheat the oven to 350°F and butter a 9x9-inch baking dish.

In a medium bowl, toss together the pear slices, lemon juice, sugar, and cinnamon.

In a separate bowl, mix together the oats, flour, brown sugar, and cinnamon.

Stir in the melted butter until the mixture is well combined.

Spread the pear mixture in the prepared baking dish and top with the oat mixture.

Bake for 45 minutes, or until the topping is golden brown and the pears are tender.

Serve warm with a scoop of vanilla ice cream, if desired.

Nutritional Information: Protein: 3g, Carbohydrate: 37g, Sugar: 22g, Sat Fat: 11g, Fiber: 4g, Fat: 11g, Calories: 270

Strawberry Sorbet

Prep Time: 10 mins, **Servings:** 4, **Cooking Time:** 0 mins

Ingredients:

- 4 cups strawberries, hulled
- 1 cup water
- ¾ cup sugar
- 2 tbsp lemon juice

Directions:

In a blender, combine the strawberries, water, sugar, and lemon juice.

Blend until smooth.

Pour the mixture into an ice cream maker and churn according to the manufacturer's instructions.

Transfer the sorbet to a freezer-safe container and freeze for at least 2 hours before serving.

Nutritional Information: Protein: 1g, Carbohydrate: 41g, Sugar: 37g, Sat Fat: 0g, Fiber: 4g, Fat: 0g, Calories: 162

Peanut Butter and Chocolate Black Bean Brownie
Prep Time: 10 mins, **Servings:** 9, **Cooking Time:** 25 mins

Ingredients:

- 1 can black beans, drained and rinsed
- 2 eggs
- ¼ cup peanut butter
- ¼ cup unsweetened cocoa powder
- ¼ cup sugar
- 1 tsp vanilla extract
- ¼ tsp salt
- ¼ tsp baking powder
- ¼ cup chocolate chips

Directions:

Preheat the oven to 350°F and grease an 8x8-inch baking pan.

In a food processor, blend the black beans, eggs, peanut butter, cocoa powder, sugar, vanilla extract, salt, and baking powder until smooth.

Stir in the chocolate chips.

Pour the mixture into the prepared pan and smooth the top with a spatula.

Bake for 25 minutes, or until the edges start to pull away from the sides of the pan and the brownie is set.

Let the brownie cool for 10 minutes before cutting into squares and serving.

Nutritional Information: Protein: 8g, Carbohydrate: 24g, Sugar: 15g, Sat Fat: 5g, Fiber: 5g, Fat: 11g, Calories: 170

Chocolate "Mousse" With Greek Yogurt And Berries

Prep Time: 5 mins, **Servings:** 4, **Cooking Time:** 0 mins

Ingredients:

- 1 cup low-fat Greek yogurt
- ¼ cup chocolate protein powder
- 1 tbsp unsweetened cocoa powder
- 1 tsp vanilla extract
- 1 cup mixed berries

Directions:

In a medium bowl, whisk together the Greek yogurt, protein powder, cocoa powder, and vanilla extract until smooth.

Divide the mixture among 4 glasses or bowls.

Top with the mixed berries and serve immediately.

Nutritional Information: Protein: 16g, Carbohydrate: 23g, Sugar: 17g, Sat Fat: 2g, Fiber: 4g,

Fat: 2g, Calories: 170

Summer Breezes Smoothie

Prep Time: 5 mins, **Servings:** 1, **Cooking Time:** 0 mins

Ingredients:

- 1 cup frozen mixed berries
- 1 banana
- 1 cup coconut water
- 1 tsp honey
- 1 tsp chia seeds

Directions:

In a blender, combine the frozen berries, banana, coconut water, honey, and chia seeds.

Blend until smooth and creamy.

Pour into a glass and serve immediately.

Nutritional Information: Protein: 3g, Carbohydrate: 34g, Sugar: 24g, Sat Fat: 0g, Fiber: 7g, Fat: 2g, Calories: 158

Mascarpone And Honey Figs

Prep Time: 5 mins, **Servings:** 4, **Cooking Time:** 0 mins

Ingredients:

- 4 figs, quartered
- 4 tbsp mascarpone cheese
- 4 tsp honey
- 1 tsp lemon zest

Directions:

Place the fig quarters on a serving plate.

Top each fig quarter with 1 tbsp of mascarpone cheese.

Drizzle with honey and sprinkle with lemon zest.

Serve immediately.

Nutritional Information: Protein: 2g, Carbohydrate: 22g, Sugar: 17g, Sat Fat: 6g, Fiber: 2g, Fat: 7g, Calories: 148

Hot Cocoa Cup

Prep Time: 5 mins, **Servings:** 1, **Cooking Time:** 5 mins

Ingredients:

- 1 cup milk
- 1 tbsp unsweetened cocoa powder
- 1 tbsp sugar
- 1 tsp vanilla extract
- 1 tsp whipped cream, for serving (optional)
- 1 tsp chocolate chips, for serving (optional)

Directions:

In a small saucepan, heat the milk over medium heat until it comes to a simmer.

Whisk in the cocoa powder, sugar, and vanilla extract until smooth.

Pour the hot cocoa into a mug and top with whipped cream and chocolate chips, if desired.

Serve immediately.

Nutritional Information: Protein: 8g, Carbohydrate: 29g, Sugar: 27g, Sat Fat: 6g, Fiber: 1g, Fat: 8g, Calories: 191

30-Day Meal Plan

Days	Breakfast	Lunch	Dinner
1	Delicious Blueberry Smoothie	Sautéed Spinach with Pumpkin Seeds	Almond Butter Chicken
2	Cranberry Hotcakes	Homestyle Bean Soup	Spiced Beef
3	Red Velvet Beet and Cherry Smoothie	Butter Bean Penne	Salmon Patties
4	Beet Berry Smoothie	Healthy Bean Soup	Amazing Grilled Chicken and Blueberry Salad
5	Cheese And Vegetable Frittata	Zucchini With Cheesy Lasagna	Za'atar Cod Fillets
6	Quinoa Vegetable Soup	Slow Cooker Quinoa Lentil Tacos	Tomato Beef
7	Raisin Cashew Oats	Lentil Veggie Stew	Crispy Trout with Herb
8	Spicy Turkey Wraps	Veggie Pea Soup	Parmesan Pork Chops
9	Muesli with Berries, Seeds, and Nuts	Butternut Soup	Roast Salmon with Tarragon
10	Chicken Meatballs	Fried Legume	Beef Tenderloin Medallions With Yogurt Sauce
11	Quinoa with Cinnamon and Peaches	Bean Curd Bake	Creamy Tuna Salad
12	German Potato Soup	Flavors Corn Soup	Chicken with Orzo and Lemon
13	Strawberry Quinoa Salad	Flavors Vegetable Stew	Sesame Beef Skewers
14	Pasta Primavera	Spaghetti Squash with Walnuts and Parmesan	Strip Steak Quinoa
15	Peach-Cranberry Sunrise Muesli	Vegetable Fruit Bowl with Lentil	Pistachio Flounder Fillets
16	Broccoli Chicken Rice	Spicy Pear Tacos	Orzo, Bean, And Tuna Salad
17	Bowl Of Guacamole And Mango With Black Beans	Sesame Spinach	Turkey Keema Curry
18	Berry Griddle Cakes	Spicy Bean Soup	Catfish with Egg Pecans
19	Berry Greek Yogurt Parfaits with Granola	Umami Mushrooms	Stewed Cod Filet with Tomatoes
20	Lemon Brussels Sprouts	Cauliflower Mashed "Potatoes"	Rosemary-Lemon Salmon
21	Avocado Tomato Salsa	Healthy Banana Cookies With Oatmeal	Best Lasagna Soup
22	Spiced Chickpeas With Peppered Parsley	Fruit & Veg Soup	Citrus Tilapia
23	Cannellini Bean Hummus	Creamy Delicious Farro	Lentil Beef Bolognese

24	Crispy Carrot Fries	Nutritious Roasted Chickpeas	Pasta with Lemon Spiced Shrimp and Cheese
25	Whipped Ricotta Toast	Cottage Cheese Mousse	Garlic Mushroom Chicken
26	Cottage Cheese Mousse	Whipped Ricotta Toast	Spicy Shrimp
27	Honey-Lime Berry Salad	Bean Curd Bake	Slow Roasted Beef
28	Thyme Mushrooms	Vegetarian Gyros	Olive Turkey Patties
29	Lentil Trail Mix	Potato Squash Soup	Mediterranean Baked Fish
30	Hummus	Fried Rice Tom Yum	Chicken Shaheata

Made in the USA
Las Vegas, NV
16 August 2023